Sex Scan of the French Music-Hall

Gaby Deslys & Harry Pilcer 1900-1920

David Bret

DbBooks

© Copyright David Bret 2020

David Bret has asserted his moral right to be identified as the Author of this Work in accordance with the Copyright Designs and Patents Act 1988.

All rights reserved. No part of this publication may be reproduced or transmitted in any form or by any means, electronic or mechanical, including photocopying, recording or any information storage or retrieval system without the prior permission in writing from David Bret.

A catalogue record for this book is available from the British Library.

ISBN: 978-1092186582

Contents:

Introduction 5
1: Gabrielle of the Lilies 6
2: The Charm of Paris 20
3: The King and the Showgirl 35
4: I'm Just Wild About Harry!.......................................62
5: When Two Worlds Collide 74
6: *Honeymoon Express* 92
7: *The Little Parisienne* 107
8: Stars of the Silent Screen..120
9: The Great War..130
10: *Stop! Look! Listen!*..145
11: *The God of Luck* 177
12: The Fading Lily 187
13: The Show Goes On 198
14: Epilogue: Berlin…and Beyond.....................211
Bibliography & Sources...221
Filmography 224

Introduction

It was known as the golden age of the music-hall—and introduced to the world an exciting range of artistes whose lives were so blatantly scandalous that they were incapable of crossing the Channel or the Atlantic without raising the hackles of the censors and moral groups. Some even raised eyebrows on home soil, in an age when France was believed to have been liberated in the wake of *La Belle Époque*. What makes these artistes of paramount importance, even the ones remembered only for a handful of songs and anecdotes, is their influence on so many of the stars of today and the recent past.

Gaby Deslys (1881-1920) was the original "Tart with a Heart", a fickle but talented young woman who achieved world fame via the casting-couch, and who maintained her legendary status by developing a unique talent for being in the wrong place at the right time, breaking hearts and dispensing with fortunes along the way, and even toppling a monarchy.

Harry Pilcer was a New Yorker of Hungarian extraction who, after an apprenticeship as a rent-boy, went on to become the most famous dancer to emerge from the United States, pre-Fred Astaire. His partnership with Gaby Deslys saw them billed as the world's greatest variety act, and enabled them to pack theatres on both sides of the Atlantic. When he later teamed up with the legendary Mistinguett, she wrote her signature tune, "Mon homme" (My Man) in his honour, having described him as the great love of her life.

Alternatively touching and shocking, dirty but delightful, this is their story…

1: Gabrielle of the Lilies

She was born in Marseille on 4 November 1881, the third daughter of Anna and Hippolyte Caire, and baptized Marie-Elise Gabrielle. In those days, the area surrounding the rue de la Rotonde was nothing like the red-light district of today. To live there at the end of the nineteenth century meant that one had achieved a certain status in life. The Caires had moved into Number 53 in 1874, a few months after their marriage, to take over the family drapery business. Hippolyte was thirty-three, Anna Terras seventeen. Besides Gaby, as she was nicknamed, there were four more children. Marie-Thérese died aged thirteen months; Léon, born in 1876, died of tuberculosis; Aimée, the family favourite, was born in 1879; Marie-Jeanne Mathilde, known as Matichon, completed the family in 1883.

Hyppolyte Caire was agoraphobic, and stingy towards the point of absurdity. Much of his work was delegated to his poorly-paid team of travelling representatives, constantly on the move throughout southern France. At home, saving money was as much of a preoccupation of making it. There were harsh economic measures regarding food, heating and cleaning: nothing was ever thrown away. Many years later, his wife remarked that the reason for Hyppolyte's tyranny stemmed from his grief over Léon's death, and the fact that he had adored his daughter Aimée, but loathed the other two.

From an early age, Gaby began displaying signs of waywardness. For this reason her father kept her at a distance from her more impressionable sisters by sending her to the nearby Convent of St Maur, a draconic institution which only succeeded in making her yearn for a more exciting way of life. She was devoted to her mother, and loved to hear her talk about the theatre and music-hall. Anna had aspired towards such a profession, but family values—her parents had drilled it into her that no decent girl ever set foot on the stage—had prevented her from pursuing her dream.

At the end of 1896, Hyppolyte transferred his business to larger premises at 52, rue Tapis-Vert. The living quarters were on the first floor, and Gaby and Matichon shared a room facing the main street. Gaby had just turned fifteen, and had decided that she would never do anything as "downgrading" as housework and raising children. Her window faced that of the brothel above one of the shops across the way, and watching the evening traffic gave her an idea. If she could not make it in the theatre, she would become a prostitute! More than this, she arranged an interview with the madam which would have involved her being "tested out" by one of the clients—and who at once informed her mother.

Rather than punish her daughter, Anna took her to an afternoon matinee at the Alcazar, one of the most popular music-halls in Marseille, though not one of the most respectable. Her logic behind this was that if she got Gaby interested in pursuing a career on the stage, she would accompany her everywhere and prevent her from getting into trouble. Topping the bill was the Algerian-born chanteuse Polaire (Emilie Marie Bouchard, 1874-1939), as known for her Spartan private life and for having been painted by Toulouse-Lautrec as she was for her over-the-top exotic costumes and 18-inch, tightly-corseted waist. Her "show-stopper" was the French version of *Ta-ra-ra-Boom-de-ay*. She at once became Gaby's favourite entertainer, a woman she would worship and emulate for the rest of her life, though they never met. Another headliner at the Alcazar, also born in Algeria, was Eugénie Buffet (1866-1934), one of the first *chanteuses-réalistes* whose signature song was Jean Varney's *Sérénade du pave*. Edith Piaf portrayed her and sang this in the 1954 film, *French Cancan*, while Marlene Dietrich's camp-follower character Amy Jolly, in the film *Morocco* (1930), was based on her.

Gaby met Buffet after the show, and asked her permission to perform *Sérénade du pave* for an audition which her mother had arranged to take place at the Alcazar, in the manager's office. The subject was one not permitted to be discussed in the Caire household—poverty. The singer stands under the woman's window, hoping that she will appear and show her charity:

> Que m'importe que tu sois belle,
> Duchesse, ou lorette aux yeux doux,
> Ou que tu laves la vaisselle?
> Pourvu que tu jettes deux sous!
>
> (What do I care if you're beautiful,
> A duchess, or a gentle-eyed courtesan,
> Or that you wash dishes?
> As long as you throw me two sous!)

Gaby failed the audition, but the song haunted her for the rest of her life and frequently cropped up in her repertoire. For now, she left the convent school, and her mother enrolled her at the Conservatoire, where she studied singing, speech and solfège. Though keen to learn as much as she could, she invariably achieved poor results in her examinations because she missed so many lessons on account of her fragile health. She would always be prone to chest-colds and bronchitis, never more so than in the winter of 1897, when much of her time was spent in bed, gazing at the brothel across the street.

The brothel continued to fascinate her and one evening—she had just turned seventeen—Gaby observed a woman undressing in front of the window. Usually, the curtains were kept closed, so as not to attract complaints from passers-by. Tonight, aware that she was being watched, the woman left them open and over the next few hours, with a succession of clients, put on what must have been an enlightening display for her inquisitive young audience. Gaby's strict Catholic upbringing should have made her feel shocked. The nuns at the convent always made the pupils turn their backs when anyone resembling a prostitute walked by the gates and the Mother Superior had complained to the authorities about the "tide of vice" in Marseille—not that this had achieved anything. As for Gaby, the next morning she borrowed money from her mother, saying that she needed this to buy books to help with her studies. What she actually bought was a pair of binoculars so that she might better study the goings-on across the way.

A few evenings later, the prostitute left the curtains open again, and Gaby recognized one of her clients. This was Ludo, the son of a doctor friend of her father's, whom Gaby had fancied for a while. The recipient of some of her confidences later in life was Régine Flory (Marie-Antoinette Artaz, 1894-1926), the music-hall star remembered today for her "ultimate performance" of June 1926— arguing over a contract in the manager's office at London's Drury Lane Theatre, before pulling a gun out of her bag and shooting herself dead. Gaby told Flory that twenty-year-old Ludo had been so utterly beautiful that she had decided to have him for herself— and to threaten him with public exposure for consorting with whores, should he reject her advances. He did not, and she confirmed to Flory how she lost her virginity "behind a wall somewhere, on my way home from class".

Ludo was not Gaby's only lover, now that she had been deflowered. There was a brief affair with an unnamed dancer, and a more serious one with Peter Lepkovitch, a former musician at the Conservatoire. Ludo was the most important, though, because he was a fellow "rebel" who had gone against his father's wishes by leaving the Conservatoire to enrol at a college for journalists. He confided to Gaby that he had important connections in Paris—influential friends who would set him up with an apartment and a job, once he had passed his exams. Gaby promised him that when that day came, she would be leaving with him—to make her name on the stage. As for now, there were a number of obstacles to overcome.

Gaby's sister Aimée had recently married another friend of the family, Jean Fleury, the son and heir of a local businessman. Then, early in 1899, Aimée died suddenly, the third of the Caires' children to succumb to tuberculosis. Her death would have a lasting effect on Hippolyte. Within a few years his entire family would have turned against him, and he would lose everything he had worked for. For the time being, he prevented Gaby from attending the Conservatoire, and she was forced to work in the drapery shop. Needless to say, when allowed to return to the institution five months later to sit her exams, she failed them all. It was now that Ludo approached Hippolyte, asking him for Gaby's hand in marriage. Far from opposing the match, he gave the couple his blessing.

Gaby returned to the Conservatoire, and at the end of June 1902 gained a diploma in solfège. In the middle of August, Ludo passed his exams, obtained a distinction in journalism, and at received an offer of employment in Paris. Though close to her mother and remaining sister Matichon, Gaby needed little tempting to leave Marseille. Under cover of darkness, trunks were smuggled into the house on the rue Tapis-Vert. Nothing untoward was suspected because the Caires took in deliveries at all hours, and Hippolyte never checked anything himself, leaving this to the morning shift. While the family were in bed, Gaby filled the trunks and they were collected the next night by Ludo's friends and taken to the left-luggage department at the Gare St-Charles.

Two mornings later, Ludo called for Gaby as usual, and breakfasted with the family. He informed them that he and Gaby had been invited to dine with college friends after their classes, and not to be concerned should it be late when he escorted her home. An hour later they boarded the express train for Paris—their luggage had been sent on ahead, and Gaby was told by Ludo that his contact in Paris had secured the keys for an apartment on the Left Bank. When the couple arrived at the Gare de Lyon, Gaby sent her parents a telegram to the effect that there was nothing to worry about: she had left home to seek fame on the stage, and a letter would follow. She did not give her address, well aware that as she was only twenty and still legally a minor—that if her parents contacted the police in Paris, Ludo could have been arrested on an abduction charge, resulting in an almost certain prison sentence, while Gaby would be forcibly returned to Marseille.

Ludo's contact was the actress Marie-Thérèse Kolb (1856-1935), with whom he had a fling—when he was fifteen and she thirty-seven, therefore more rule-breaking—when she had visited the Marseille Conservatoire while appearing in a play in the city. The "apartment" was a tawdry room in the aptly-named Hôtel l'Amour in the 9th arrondissement, and the couple moved in as man and wife. Here, their problems began. Though she had little money and was relying entirely on Ludo supporting her, Gaby refused to compromise. No would-be star should be expected to suffer sleepless nights because of a noisy, over-used lavatory cistern, she declared, nor put up with the stench coming from the lidless grate directly under her window. Thus she set off for Kolb's own plush apartment, which *was* on the Left Bank, to give her a piece of her mind for conning her. Kolb surprised her by declaring that Ludo himself had organized their lodgings, and when Gaby burst into tears upon hearing this, the actress cheered her up by announcing that her friend Eugene Rouzier-Dorcières, the assistant director of the Olympia Music-Hall, was looking for chorus girls, and that she would put in a good word for her. What she did not let on was *how* he auditioned them...

Gaby turned up wearing the chinchilla wrap she had purloined from her mother's wardrobe—and with her mid-length blonde hair in tight little curls. Rouzier-Dorcières was smitten, and when he asked Gaby to define her speciality—he meant whether she danced or sang—she retorted, "Anything, so long as the price is right!" With this she removed her wrap, and when the assistant director had taken in her voluptuous hour-glass figure, he nodded to the couch in the corner of his office. Gaby complied and afterwards executed a song-and-dance routine. Rouzier-Dorcières approved, offered her a small part in his next revue, and told her to report for rehearsals later in the week.

The Olympia revue was not to be, as over the next few days Gaby played the field, offering herself and her as yet unproved talents to a number of younger, more attractive theatrical entrepreneurs—without success. Undeterred, she enrolled for lessons with Madame Paravicini, one of the most respected drama-coaches in turn-of-the-century Paris, and one of the most expensive. To pay for her tuition, she accepted whatever work was on offer, singing and dancing in the lesser-known and less respectable music-halls and *café-concerts* around Belleville-Ménilmontant. Such engagements did not pay well, and neither did they enhance her already racy reputation, though she always managed to leave on the arm of a wealthy admirer. If Gaby Caire had any class at all, it was related to the fact that she only chose the good-looking ones, and not the elderly lechers favoured by some of her contemporaries—which enabled her to at least *think* that she was behaving respectably.

Madame Paravicini's motto was, "Bring me a nun, and I will

turn her into an actress." She certainly did well with Gaby, while turning a blind eye to her *demimondaine* activities. Within a week she found her a position in the chorus of *Y'a des surprises*, which opened on 9 October 1902 at the Parisiana, a café-concert on the boulevard Poissonnière. She was billed simply as "Gaby", and there is no record of what she actually did. Suffice to say, such was her reputation for being *une baise facile* (an easy lay) that within a month she had amassed a sizeable collection of jewels and furs. One evening, Polaire turned up at the theatre, intent on seeing what all the fuss was about. Inside the foyer she was stopped by a reporter who asked her opinion of the young woman whose picture was pinned to the wall. Pointing to the stole draped about Gaby's shoulders, she barked before promptly heading back to her carriage, "Any woman who wears mink is nothing but a common tart!"

While appearing at the Parisiana, Gaby caught the attention of Jules Berny, the director of the Théâtre des Maturins. He had written a song, *Je chante la gloire de la Parisienne*, and a sketch had been drafted around this by his friend Jacques-Charles (Charles-Jacques Mardochée, 1882-1971)—later hailed as the greatest revue writer of his generation. Berny engaged Gaby, and Jacques-Charles wrote several more sketches and came up with a two-hour show, *La Parisienne*. On the face of it, they were taking a considerable risk investing capital in a little-known actress from Marseille—attempting to play a woman who had lived in Paris all her life, and in a thick accent hardly anyone could understand!

La Parisienne opened in February 1903, and was an instant hit. Gaby also effected another name change. The posters outside the theatre now hailed her as "Deslys", but this would soon be amended to Gaby Deslys. The name was the brainchild of an admirer who had photographed her standing in front of a flower-stall at the Gare d'Austerlitz—"Gabrielle of the Lilies". But if this was the name with which she would achieve world fame, there would be another before the final metamorphosis.

Such was the popularity of the revue that it was extended several times and, towards the end of the run, one of those felicitating her in her dressing-room after the show was a wealthy, middle-aged official from the Russian Embassy. His name was Niska and in order to please him—and keep the money coming in—Gaby changed her name to Niska Deslys. His first gift to her was a heavy string of pearls which by today's standards would have been worth several thousand pounds. A few days later, he set her up with her first apartment, a far cry from the squalid room at the Hôtel l'Amour where Ludo was left to sulk and probably regret ever bringing her to Paris. Niska filled this with valuable works of art and antique furniture, yet Gaby refused to acknowledge and appreciate his kindness. She had achieved the first of many goals, and if the couple were seen at Maxim's most nights of the week after the show, Gaby was only stringing him along until she found someone else to keep her in the luxury she had quickly become accustomed to. Though not a great deal is known about these formative years, what evidence has survived does not present her in a very favourable light.

At the end of the year, Madame Paravicini put Gaby into *Mam'zelle Chichi*, by M. C. Esquier and Henri Christiné, one of the foremost songwriters of the day. This opened at the Scala on 27 January 1904, though Gaby was not the star of the show. This was Émilienne d'Alençon (c1870-1945), one of the most notorious *horizontalistes* in Paris. This fascinating woman had made her stage debut at the Cirque d'Été in 1889, with a troupe of tinted, performing rabbits. Halfway through her act her flimsy, tight-fitting bodice had given way, since which time she had not looked back. Her roster of lovers past and present was exhaustive, and included King Léopold II of Belgium. She was married to the

English jockey Percy Woodland, who had won the Grand National the previous year, but was never faithful to him. Besides offering her charms to the highest bidder, pretty much like Gaby, Emilienne was something of a psycho-analyst but by all accounts, to those she chose to favour, a thoughtful, warm-hearted woman. She manipulated men, she told Gaby, because her father had manipulated her and her mother and made her childhood miserable. Her motto was, "Get as much out of the man as you can, and then show him the door!" Over the next few years, Gaby would use this maxim to its greatest advantage. For now, she took her friend's advice and ditched Niska. She kept the apartment, raising the money to pay the rent and to main her extravagant standard of living by selling some of the works of art he had bought—and by selling herself.

There followed a brief stint in *La Nouvelle Revue* at the Théâtre Marigny, where the *meneuse de revue* (star of the show) was Arlette Dorgère (1880-1965), with whom Gaby would cross swords in the not too distant future. She played a soldier who put on drag to become Mam'zelle Michel. Next she returned to the Scala to take over Émilienne d'Alençon's role in *Mam'zelle Chichi*. In her pleasant but high-pitched soprano and dressed as a pugilistic kindergarten pupil, she performed a vulgar ditty, "Les yeux en boule":

> Je veux pocher tes yeux en boule,
> Viens-donc, si t'as d'l'estomac!
>
> (I would like to blacken your eyes,
> Come on then, if you have the guts!)

The great tragi-comic *diseuse* Yvette Guilbert (1865-1944) was playing in Paris at the time, and might have got away with such a ridiculous song. Not so Gaby, who was whistled at (*the* supreme insult in France at this time) and booed off the stage—not just because of her "wooden" delivery but on account of her almost incomprehensible Marseille accent. Curiously, she attributed her failure to her age—the fact that, two months off her twenty-first birthday, she considered herself too old to be a chorus-girl and should never have been expected to perform such a childish routine in the first place. Therefore, when fired by the director of the Scala, she "docked" four years off her age—four years which would never be added back on. This caused problems for Ludo when Gaby began telling everyone they had been lovers for four years—in effect, giving the impression that she had been sleeping with him since the age of sixteen. Ludo was further aggrieved to learn how many times she had hopped on to the casting-couch. Without even saying goodbye he returned to Marseille, and no doubt repeated the events of the last eighteen months to Gaby's father—not that this would have made matters any worse, for Hippolyte Caire had sworn a solemn oath never to speak to her again on account of her reprehensible behaviour and the fact that she had brought shame on the family name.

Polaire

Eugénie Buffet

Régine Flory

Gaby in *La nouvelle revue*.

As Mam'zelle Michel in
La nouvelle revue.

2: The Charm of Paris

In December 1904, when Gaby opened in *A fleur de peau*, still at the Scala, her co-star was Ferdinand Gabin, father of actor Jean. The critics observed that her dancing had improved. Her singing had not, but would get better. Some critics made comparisons with Mistinguett. The major difference between Gaby and Miss, however, was that the latter was unashamed of her working class background, and despite her immense wealth never strayed far from her roots. For the first thirty years of her life, Gaby was an insufferable snob who, when not performing or rehearsing, spent much of the rest of the time socializing and adding to her fortune. As will be seen, it was only during the last decade of her life that she changed.

A few days after the premiere, Gaby paid her first visit to a photographer's studio. Here, apart from one study for which she wore Niska's pearls, she eschewed the usual *demimondaine* poses in exotic gowns and jewels—going one step further by wrapping a silk sheet around her naked body, and lying face-down on a bearskin rug. The picture was mass-produced, and became one of the most sought-after pin-ups in turn-of-the-century France. One journalist who saw it in a shop window commented, "Gaby Deslys is the most alluring creature ever to have graced a French stage. She is a Snow Queen!" Jacques-Charles, who boasted for many years that *he* had discovered Gaby—when in fact she had discovered herself—quaintly described her in his memoirs:

> Gaby was a loveable blonde doll, with hair as curly as a six-month-old lamb. She was rather small, with a rounded figure…pink as a Boissier fondant, with big blue eyes and an adorable mouth just like a ripe strawberry!

One of the visitors to Gaby's dressing-room during the run of *A la fleur de peau* was another young Russian, Alexandre-Pierre Guitry (1885-1957). The son of the actor Lucien, he and Gaby are not thought to have been lovers, but she was awarded the "privilege" of meeting him, which in his snobbish world seems to have amounted to something. As Sacha Guitry he would become one of France's most distinguished actor- screenwriter-directors—and with five marriages all to his protégés and countless affairs, one of the country's most notorious womanizers.

When the revue closed, Gaby moved into an apartment on the rue Constantinople, just behind the Gare Saint-Lazare. The press reported how her new armchairs and sofas were covered with cloth-of-gold to match the exquisite décor of her salon. The bill for this amounted to around £120,000 in today's money, which gives some indication not of how much she was earning—the huge salaries would come later—but how much her lovers were willing to fork out for the privilege of bedding her. There were also three maids, and a muscular homosexual manservant whose duties included running her bath, then spending one hour each evening massaging and licking her feet. Gaby paid him well, but treated him like a lackey because of his sexual preferences. Unlike many of the *horizontalistes* and *chanteuse-réalistes*, whose appeal to gay audiences formed a greater part of their success, Gaby loathed any good-looking young man unable or unwilling to yield to her nymphomaniac desires. There was of course no shortage of suitors—so many that when one left on a morning. another was waiting in the lobby to take his place. Sometimes Gaby never bothered asking the man's name—so long as a piece of jewellery or a roll of banknotes was left on the cabinet next to the bed, she did not care who she slept with. Eventually, one of these walked off with her manservant.

On 10 May 1905, Gaby opened in *Au music-hall*, staged at the

Olympia by co-directors Victor de Cottens and H. B. Marinelli. Anna and Matichon Caire travelled up from Marseille for the premiere, and stayed at her apartment. She compered the first half, and performed five songs after the interval. It was not her vocal talents but her soubrette uniform—garters, silk stockings, high-buttoned boots, hat trimmed with ostrich feathers, and a short dress which revealed more cleavage than most considered decent—that got her noticed by a wealthy, forty-something Japanese businessman sitting in one of the boxes. His name was Sessue Hayakawa (no relation to the Hollywood actor of the same name) and when Gaby met him in her dressing room after the show she detected "from the cut of his suit" that he would make an ideal lover and benefactor. Needless to say he spent several nights at the apartment on the rue de Constantinople.

Hayakawa was the first of Gaby's men *not* to want to be seen in public with a music-hall artiste, insisting their affair remain a closely-guarded secret. Gaby agreed to this, for a price—he bought her a car, her first, a cream and white Brougham, one of the first to appear in Paris. For a while she was thrilled at the clandestine meetings following the hastily-scribbled notes handed over by an intermediary. In the end, her need to put on a public display got the better of her, and she got Hayakawa's chauffeur to drive them around Paris, and eventually to the racetrack at Auteuil. Gaby loved going to the races, though she was shrewd enough never to bet her own money on the horses. The appeal was catching up with the latest fashion trends, hats especially. Gaby was a precursor of the outrageous Ascot aficionado, Gertrude Schilling—the bigger the hat, the more important the wearer was made to feel. She designed many of her own using the tail feathers of egrets, birds-of-paradise, and some of the rarer species which came close to extinction because of the client's latest whim. When George Cukor made *My Fair Lady*, sixty years later, he suggested to Cecil Beaton that Audrey Hepburn should resemble Gaby as much as possible during the famous Ascot scene. In fact, this featured a number of Gaby's actual creations.

It was at Auteuil that summer that Gaby met Liane de Pougy (Anne Marie de Chassaigne, 1869-1950), the most controversial courtesan and *meneuse de revue* of them all. Openly bisexual, she had made her debut at the Folies-Bergère in 1896, dressed as a golden spider in *L'araignée d'or*, written by Jean Lorrain, who had escorted her just about everywhere since. Lorrain (Paul Alexandre Duval, 1855-1906) was a gay poet, journalist and writer of decadent novels, and never content unless evoking a scandal. Though he covered much literary ground during his life, he hated working, preferring to spend his leisure time picking up sailors along the Marseille, Nice, Brest and Paris waterfronts. He wrote in his memoirs, "Fucking is basically a sport for idle minds. When one is working, it's goodbye to arse!" He was equally at home strutting along the boulevards wearing the latest dandy fashion, or going out in drag. He was a drug-addict and, when he met Gaby he was suffering from the ravages of syphilis—the disease which killed him the following year.

The previous day, Liane de Pougy had sent Gaby a *billet-doux*, arranging to meet her—solely with the intention of luring her away from Hayakawa. When she saw Lorrain—wearing a bleached blonde wig and full make-up, and with a young sailor clinging to his arm, she turned on her heels and made a hasty exit. This incurred Lorrain's wrath, and the next day *he* sent Gaby a note, threatening to expose her affair with Hayakawa to the press unless she met up with de Pougy and apologized for *her* behaviour! Gaby went to see the courtesan, who was waiting for a visit from her current lover—whose name, she told Gaby, she had forgotten. Gaby was invited into her boudoir and stayed long enough to ask why there were so many emerald rings in the glass dish next to the bed. De Pougy explained: beginning with her left foot, the man in her life would "by way of mouth" place a ring on each of the toes, then in the same manner transfer them to the other foot as a preliminary to love-making. She got her apology from Gaby, who had done nothing to be sorry for, but when she tried to seduce her, Gaby shrugged off her advances and left. Lorrain exacted his revenge a few days later, in his weekly newspaper column. He could not name Gaby Deslys' latest "victim" for fear of litigation, he wrote, though he *could* reveal that he was a high-ranking Japanese governmental official.

By the end of 1905 Gaby's relationship with Sessue Hayakawa had cooled somewhat, but he was intent on keeping his pretty little *cocotte* for as long as possible. He bought her an apartment in the rue Balny d'Avricourt, near the Étoile where, despite the opulence of the area most of her neighbours were upper-class whores. Hayakawa had been unaware of this, and his first visit to the apartment would be his last. He told her their affair was over, but Gaby was unperturbed. He may have paid for the apartment, but so as to hide this from his business associates he had purchased it in her name. She "celebrated" her freedom by going to the auction room at Drouot and—using the money Hayakawa had paid her for their "farewell fuck"—purchased several items of Louis XV furniture. She also hired another manservant-masseur, this time one who was not gay—the interview took place in her bedroom.

In February 1906, still at the Olympia, Gaby opened in *Paris-fêtard*, where her co-star was Julia Searle, a popular transvestite entertainer of the day. The highlight of the show was a dance called *La kraquette*. One evening the performance was halted when the theatre was invaded by placard-waving suffragettes chanting, "We pay taxes too! We want the vote!" Minutes after the curtain came down, Gaby joined their protest outside on the boulevard des Capucines.

In March, Gaby appeared in *Que tu dis?* at the Cigale, in Montmartre. She did not get along with the manager, Max Viterbo, who fired her. As luck would have it, during her final performance she found herself another admirer—one interested in her act rather than in wanting to sleep with her. British actor and theatre manager George Grossmith (1874-1935) was on a talent-scouting trip to Paris looking for "exotic turns" for George Edwardes' production of *The New Aladdin*, written by James Tolman Tanner and scheduled to open at London's Gaiety Theatre on 29 September. Edwardes already had the leads: Grossmith was to play the Genie of the Lamp. The other cast members included Harry Grattan, who also choreographed the tableaux, as Ebenezer—and Adrienne Augard as the Princess. The principal boy—whose name was shortened to Lally—was Gertie Millar. Initially, Goldsmith wanted Gaby to play the part of the Princess's French maid, but she objected, declaring how "The Charm of Paris" would not be seen dead playing a "midinette"—and that in any case, the fee Edwardes proposed was not worth the horrors of travelling on a boat across the Channel. Goldsmith returned to London, expecting Edwardes to ask him to search elsewhere for his French maid. Instead, he asked Tanner to amend the script to accommodate a new character—"The Charm of Paris", as Gaby had so arrogantly baptized herself!

Gaby arrived in London at the end of August 1906. She had put the apartment on the rue Balny d'Avricourt on the market, leaving her mother in charge of the sale. In George Edwardes' office, she signed a three-month contract, but he was confident after seeing the size of the crowds welcoming her in Dover and at Victoria Station that this would be extended. She was provided with a modest suite at the Carlton Hotel, and given a weekly allowance "to tide her over" until the production opened. She had managed to persuade Edwardes to add a clause to her contract—

that she would not have to pronounce one word in English, as she did not want to make a fool of herself. She did learn two songs to be sung phonetically: *The English Language*, and the ridiculously-titled *When In Summertime I Go To Some Place Mondaine*. *Sur la plage* and *Le Charme de Paris*, would be performed in French and English. All were pure drivel, made worse by the fact that no one could understand what she was singing about—in either language.

The production was fraught with problems. Gertie Millar's husband, Lionel Monckton, had composed much of the score. When he fell seriously ill, Millar dropped out to look after him, and was replaced by Lily Elsie, who most of the cast could not stand. Towards the end of the first run, Monckton recovered. Elsie was fired, and Millar reinstated. The critics and the audiences, however, were only interested in Gaby Deslys, who made a sensational entrance when Lally rubbed his magic lamp and asked the Genie for "all the charm of Paris". Arising from a wicker basket of roses, she wore the same short, flouncy costume that had caused the Olympia audiences to catch their breath. For ten minutes, the air was rent with cheers and wolf-whistles, and these continued throughout her opening number.

What really drove London audiences wild was *The Jiu-Jitsu Waltz*, choreographed by Gaby herself with S. K. Eida (1878-1918), an instructor with the Japanese School of Jujitsu, situated in Oxford Street. How Gaby met him is not known. They became lovers, and remained so until shortly after the revue closed. At 5 feet 6 inches, he was not as tall as Gaby and was nicknamed "The Pocket Hercules". Rough-and-ready does not even begin to describe the routine, which ended with Eida tossing her into the air several times and with her making a perfect landing each time until the couple collapsed in a heaving heap in the middle of the stage.

Sur la plage was another matter. The sketch had been created to allow Gaby to flaunt herself at the men in the audience—her bathing-suit exposing her shoulders and much of her ample cleavage, and she had fastened two silver starfish over her breasts. Walking up to the front of the stage she sang:

> When I take my *bain-de-mer*,
> At *what* do the men all stare?

On the evening of the premiere, some members of the audience walked out in disgust—and of course, when this was reported in the newspapers so many people were turned away from the box-office that the show, which should have closed at the end of December, was three times extended until the end of April 1907. In all, there were 203 performances. Photographs of Gaby in her bathing-suit took up full pages in *The Tatler* and *The Sketch*. She received undisclosed but said to be huge fees for advertising *Odol* mouthwash and *Pears* soap. *The Times*' critic observed:

> The artistes are amateurs, the dances are too brief, the songs are second-rate, and Lily Elsie even more disappointing than usual. Miss Gaby Deslys, recently imported to make London gay, is the only one who is enticing!

The *Daily Telegraph* enthused of Gaby:

> She is the perfect incarnation of The Charm of Paris. She is dressed as in a dream, her gait is as pungent as it is fascinating, and the bathing suit that she wears in *The English Language* is fascinating!

As in Paris, Gaby was besieged with male admirers. She was told by George Edwardes *not* to accept gifts from men, and aware of her reputation he hired a "personal assistant" to ensure that decency prevailed. Away from the theatre, things were different. When *Aladdin* closed, Gaby planned on staying in London, convinced she would be offered another revue by one of the managers she had "fraternized" with. Dismissing *The Jiu-Jitsu Waltz* as a novelty, she began taking dance lessons with Will Bishop, a respected tutor who began his career in 1893 dancing and choreographing sketches for the Empire Theatre, in Leicester Square—also managed by Edwardes. Gaby's association with Bishop was strictly platonic—he was gay, and made it clear to her that he never had been and never would be sexually interested in women. The two became friends, and for a while she was *his* sponsor, financing his frequent trips between London and Paris until 1909, when he was appointed director of dance with the Berlin Metropol. All that she asked for in return was the occasional "refresher" lesson, to keep her dancing up to scratch.

In May 1907 Gaby returned to Paris. Her mother had sold the apartment on the rue Balny d'Avricourt and found her a small house at 3, rue Henri-de-Bornier, near the Bois de Boulogne, which she would always refer to, in English, as "Number Three". At 160,000 francs, this cost almost twice the amount that Gaby had budgeted for—not that this presented her with a problem, as she made up the difference by selling some of the jewels given to her by admirers. The Cigale's Max Viterbo, who had fired her from *Que tu dis?* had travelled to London to see her, and had been so shocked by how *good* she was that he wrote a piece for *Le Parisien* questioning her authenticity. "People who knew her before are asking themselves if this is the same Gaby from a few years ago," he wrote, and to make a point suggested she should be examined by a doctor—so convinced was he that she was an impostor, and that the real Gaby had returned to Marseille!

Gaby headed for Viterbo's office, intent on giving him a piece of her mind—and was surprised when by way of an apology he offered her a lucrative fee to partner Max Déarly in *Tu veux rire*, at Les Ambassadeurs, the café-concert which he also managed on the avenue Gabriel. Déarly (1874-1943) was as renowned for his bad temper as for his craft. Even so, Gaby did not hesitate when Madame Paravicini asked her to work with him, particularly as Mistinguett had turned down the revue. From now on, the great star would despise her—and before very long, so would Déarly.

Born Lucien Rolland, in Paris, this extraordinary man began dancing at sixteen. He acquired his stage name while touring with the Scottish revue artist Mac Deely—asked to replace him at the top of the bill when he fell ill, he stole the limelight, and Deely's name, adapting it only slightly. As Max Déarly, he made his Paris debut at the Ba-ta-clan in 1900. An eccentric comedian, with an equine face and deadpan delivery, he was also an agile dancer and capable mimic, offering spot-on impersonations of the big stars of the day—Mayol, Dranem, and Mistinguett whom he later partnered and hated even more than Gaby.

The revue opened on 21 June 1907, and Gaby and Déarly's screaming matches before and after every performance had everyone running for cover. What Déarly loathed most about his tetchy, wayward co-star was the way she upstaged him by flaunting herself at the audience—showering them with hundreds of bunches of tiny rosebuds each night after the finale. He was further infuriated by the flamboyant homosexuals always found loitering around the door of her dressing-room. Though only a short while ago Gaby had professed to disliking any man "incapable of satisfying a woman's desires", she now encouraged them. As such, she became Europe's first gay icon. And the song that had audiences whooping standing on their seats was her attack of the England that had made her a star:

L'Angleterre est un beau pays,
Mais j'aime beaucoup mieux la France…
De presque tout de c'qu'il a chez nous,
Ils n'en ont pas en Angleterre!
De l'autre côté du Détroit les hommes nous sont austères…

(England is a beautiful country,
But I like France much more...
Everything we have here,
They don't have in England!
On the other side of the Straits the men are austere to us…)

Tu veux rire broke all the box-office records at Les Ambassadeurs. The run was extended several times. Then, in the middle of September Gaby dropped out of the revue and no explanation was given why, or why she suddenly left Paris. There was speculation that the nightly rows with Max Déarly had become too much for her—also, that she had collapsed from exhaustion in her dressing-room, and that her doctor had advised her to rest. In fact, she travelled to London where she had been booked for a season at the Alhambra, in Leicester Square. The director, Alfred Moul, had seen her dancing *The Jiu-Jitsu Waltz* at the Gaiety Theatre, and he put her into the second half of a bill which included the operetta, *Les Cloches de Corneville*. She had two spots. The first was a song-and-dance routine, *La journée d'une Parisienne*, choreographed by her friend Will Bishop. The second saw her playing Diabolo—the latest craze which involved balancing a double-headed spinning-top thrown up and caught on a tautened string attached to two sticks—all this while dressed as an Egyptian mummy sheathed in silk. As she worked her way through the 15-

minute routine, this unwound to reveal a low cut bathing-suit similar to the one she had worn in *The New Aladdin*, and the men in the audience went wild.

Gaby spent the Christmas of 1907 in London, the first time she had been away from France during the festive season. An incident was reported in the press, when an unnamed English lord attempted to seduce her in her dressing-room. She spurned his advances, and as she was leaving the theatre he flung himself under the wheels of her carriage. He was not badly hurt but Winston Churchill, who could not stand her, debated the matter in the House of Commons.

Les Cloches de Corneville closed early in January, and Gaby returned to Paris to prepare for her next revue, *Son Altesse l'Amour*, to be staged at the Moulin Rouge. In this she was partnered by an English revue artiste called Fred Wright. One of the visitors to her dressing-room after the show was a 35-year-old Argentinian entrepreneur named Mariano Unzué Baudrix. Gaby fell for him in a big way, and little wonder—on the evening of their first "rendez-vous" he divulged that he was a millionaire property investor. Her biographer Guy de Bellet observed, "With her Argentinian millionaire, the Queen of the Theatre now had her very own private Minister of Finance." And *how* she would use him! When she lied to him that she was only *renting* Number Three and only wished that she could own it, such was Mariano's infatuation that he did not hesitate to give her the 160,000 francs she claimed she needed to buy the place.

Mariano wanted to move into Number Three, but Gaby would not hear of this—her mother and sister Matichon were still living here. He therefore rented a plush apartment on the boulevard Malesherbes, and this became their love-nest for a while, with Mariano paying Gaby a monthly retainer of 15,000 francs. Cracks began appearing in their relationship when he wanted her to give up the stage and marry him. She *almost* conceded to his request, until receiving an offer she could hardly refuse. Max Déarly and Mistinguett had been contracted to appear at the Moulin Rouge in *Par-dessus les moulins*, and the premiere set for 16 October—but there were problems.

Mistinguett (Jeanne-Marie Bourgeois, 1875-1956) would never have anything positive to say about Gaby—indeed about any of her contemporaries and music-hall rivals. Born in Enghien, just outside Paris, she started off selling flowers and at eighteen was an "added attraction" at the Eldorado. As "La Miss" she became the toast of Paris. In a career spanning sixty years her temper and parsimony became almost as famous as her panache of plumes, exotic costumes, and a clutch of songs delivered in a quaint, inimitable style. She was also the unsung heroine of two world wars, and as such, when she died she was laid in state at the Madeleine. When Max Déarly dropped out of *Par-dessus les moulins* after a massive row with his co-star, Mistinguett refused to be partnered by a replacement and did the same. The fact that Gaby not only replaced her but scored a triumph during the brief season would stick in the older star's craw for years.

Several minor revues followed, including a non-musical one at Les Ambassadeurs where Gaby portrayed "gentleman thief", Arsène Lupin. She received a second offer from the British impresario, Alfred Moul. On condition that she make an attempt to improve her English, he was willing to put her into her own revue at the Alhambra, this time topping the bill. The next day she hired an English teacher—who of course had to be handsome and muscular, and willing to take Mariano's place in her bed when he was out of town and apparently with his approval. The trio celebrated her latest good fortune by heading for the Auteuil racetrack. What happened there that afternoon in July 1909 would have a profound effect on her for the rest of her life.

The "rug" photograph.

Gaby, in 1905.

As "The Charm of Paris"

That "outrageous" bathing costume, though today one wonders what all the fuss was about!

3: The King & The Showgirl

Gaby said of her meeting with 19-year-old Manuel of Portugal that he was the most beautiful man she had ever seen. And when he asked her to remove her hat so that he could better study her face, the chemistry between them was instant.

The king had arrived in Paris a few days earlier on an unofficial visit. With him was his "guardian angel"—José-Maria, Marquess of Lavradio (José Maria do Espírito Santo de Almeida Corrêa de Sá, 1874—1945), who had saved his life during his father's assassination, and who had sworn never to leave his side save for when he was in his room, safely asleep. His French public relations officer and guide throughout the visit was one Madame de Téval. When Manuel asked her to organize a trip around Paris to see the monuments, her response was that there were just two of real significance: the race-track at Auteuil, and Gaby Deslys. Manuel was fond of gambling, and he had also seen the photograph of Gaby lying on the bearskin rug. Madame de Téval opted to kill two birds with one stone, and a message was sent to Gaby by way of the Portuguese ambassador.

Gaby was initially reluctant to meet Manuel. She disliked being told what to do, and had never been interested in "pimply youths". A man, she once said, was of no use to her unless he had hair on his chest and money in his wallet, though she was assured that Manuel would not be lacking where the latter was concerned. What Mariano Unzué and Gaby's English teacher and "stand-in" stud made of the situation is not on record. One assumes that any conversation took place in English or French for neither Gaby nor her companions knew a word of Portuguese. Neither did Mariano make an impression on the king, standing a few paces behind Gaby, holding her Pomeranian dog on a pink silk cushion!

Manuel was no pimply-faced adolescent. He was six-feet tall, handsome and muscular, fair-haired and blue-eyed, and had already had several love affairs. Though this initial meeting was formal, arrangements were made—by Madame Téval—for Gaby and Manuel to meet again, in private in her hotel suite, before he returned to Lisbon. Guy de Bellet observed:

> Manuel sank to his knees and buried his nose into her lap. She ran her fingers through his blond hair, then the Prince did what all the other men in her life had done. He carried her to the couch, and positioned her there for sentimental exchanges. Gaby protested feebly, then there was a lot of groaning as they engaged in the oldest game in the world. Was it this coupling with a Prince of royal blood that brought her untold joy? Was it her partner's youth awakening within her all the joys of spring? Whatever it was, Gaby Deslys, Snow Princess, said she felt the earth move for the first time in ages.

In September, meanwhile, Gaby was contracted to appear in *Sans rancune* at the Théâtre des Capucines. It was by two of the greatest institutions of the day, P. L. Flers and Georges Thenon, who worked under the pseudonym "Rip", and would be her most daring so far. Her co-star was to be 21-year-old Maurice Chevalier, currently the lover of Mistinguett. When Gaby learned that he and Miss were going through a trial separation, she attempted to seduce Chevalier by insisting that the preliminary rehearsals for their sketches in the new revue take place at her home. Chevalier, well aware of her unorthodox tactics, dropped out of the production.

The revue opened on 7 October and proved a sensation. The costumes were by Paul Poiret (1879-1944), the most popular, and expensive, costume designer in France. As well as dressing Gaby, Mistinguett, Joséphine Baker and Alice Delysia he later designed a black-décor, windowless room for the American dancer Isadora Duncan. In one tableau Gaby played a *demi-vierge*—a turn-of-the-century term for a woman who behaves provocatively, but without losing her virginity—with her entire body wrapped in ropes of pearls. In another, draped in furs and riding on a horse-drawn sleigh, she was a Russian princess.

Sans rancune was still drawing in the crowds at the end of November, when Manuel arrived in Paris, this time on an *official* state visit. Again he was accompanied by José-Maria Lavradio. President Fallières welcomed them at the Port Dauphine. Paris had been hit by a dustman's strike, and a huge crowd clambered over mountains of rubbish to catch a glimpse of their royal visitor. The cavalcade moved on to the Elysée Palace, and after luncheon there was a pilgrimage to Napoléon's tomb at Les Invalides, followed by an impromptu visit to the Louvre, where Manuel scribbled a note to his lover, and had this dispatched to Number Three with a huge basket of red roses. Much of the evening was spent listening to *Manon* at the Opéra—doubtless the king was bored by this, and looking forward to returning to the Hôtel Bristol, where he knew Gaby would be waiting for him. She was, having parked her car in the shadows near the back entrance—it was here, with the chauffeur sitting in the front and with the shades pulled down, that they made love.

A few evenings later, *Sans rancune* celebrated its hundredth performance. After the show, Gaby took Manuel home with her, and he stayed the night, despite the presence of Anna Caire, though Mariano did make himself scarce. And for the second time, she duped a lover, the one she claimed would remain the love of her life—by telling Manuel the same story she had told Mariano. Guy de Bellet explained:

King Manuel placed large sums of money at her disposal, conned into paying for a house that had already been bought by someone else. She then asked him for money for the furnishings. Thus every chair, every painting and every trinket was paid for twice.

Manuel had recently turned twenty, and he appears to have worked out Gaby's real age—that she was twenty-eight, and not twenty-four as promoted in her publicity material. According to one story, she joked that if she *was* "old enough to be his mother", then she had better act accordingly—and allow him to suckle her breast! The press had picked up on their affair, and though nothing was reported just yet, Gaby and Manuel were so head-over-heels in love that neither cared about public opinion. He also taught her his favourite Portuguese *fado*, "Amor sou tua", which she had translated into French:

> Antonio m'offrit un oeillet a la sorti du sermon,
> J'ai mis l'oeillet dans mon sein,
> Et Antonio dans mon coeur…
>
> (Antonio gave me a carnation after the sermon,
> I placed the carnation in my bosom,
> And Antonio in my heart…)

Antonio was of course Manuel, whose first gift to her—and there would be many more—was a heart-shaped brooch encrusted with rubies. This was placed in a silver casket decorated with rubies and lapis lazuli—the only costly knick-knack that Gaby ever bought for herself—along with the king's love-letters. He made a promise to write to her twice each week after he returned to Lisbon, which he kept.

Astonishingly, Gaby was still having a physical relationship with Mariano, though not for much longer. He had made arrangements to return to Argentina, and unselfishly hoped that *Manuel* would ask Gaby to marry him, and give up the stage. Her doctors had already warned her that she was working too hard, not taking enough breaks between revues, and that sooner rather than later her fickle health would cause major problems. What Gaby was as yet unaware of was the power that Manuel's mother swayed over him. Queen Amália (Amélia of Orléans, 1865-1951) was the eldest daughter of Philippe, Prince of Paris and Marie-Isabelle d'Orléans, but had actually been born in Twickenham, London. She was close to the British royal family, and was currently negotiating with a number of noble European houses to find her son a suitable bride. Such was Manuel's fear of her that, when the time came, he knew that he would be compelled to obey her.

A few evenings later, Manuel and Gaby went for a stroll in the Bois de Boulogne. It was the first time in years that he had worn "ordinary" clothes, and he instructed his driver, who dropped them off at the gates, to wait there until they returned. The couple ended up at a restaurant in the Pré Catalan, the picturesque spot in the middle of the Bois. Here they were recognized by the *maître de l'hôtel*, who was bribed to keep quiet. When Manuel ordered champagne, he was told that there were two Jersey cows in the stable and that their milk, warmed and spiced, would be more beneficial to Gaby's health. The *maître de l'hôtel* supplied the couple with a bucket, and after milking the cow they made love in the straw. Afterwards, post-coital, Manuel asked her to marry him. Gaby accepted, knowing nothing of royal protocol. A few days later, Manuel left for Lisbon, and Mariano sailed for Argentina. José-Maria Lavradio stayed put, waiting for the summons from Manuel to escort Gaby to Lisbon for her wedding. Anna Caire had planned to return to Marseille, but now changed her mind.

The summons arrived in February 1910, by way of an official request sanctioned by Dowager Queen Amália, who knew nothing of the true nature of her son's "friendship" with this Parisian showgirl, for Gaby to represent France in an international charity gala, to be held in Lisbon, to support the families of hundreds of victims who had recently died in a major fire in Porto. The journey from Paris took two days. Travelling overnight to Biarritz, Gaby and José-Maria Lavradio were met by several of Manuel's trusted friends who accompanied them to the Spanish-Portuguese border where they stayed at a country inn, then on to Lisbon where Gaby was installed at the Palais de Las Neccessitades, a former convent in the Ajuda district. Manuel had used this before for discreet rendez-vous with women, though Gaby was not to know this.

The gala took place at the Teatro Nacional de São Carlos on 3 March. Gaby had a 15-minute spot. She performed one of the routines from *Sans rancune*, and sang two songs, one of which was "La Parisienne". The day after the show, Queen Amália travelled to Biarritz, where she was hoping to seal a marriage contract between her son and Princess Patricia of Connaught, the grand-daughter of Queen Victoria. While here, she learned of Gaby's earlier visit to the town, and the real reason for her trip to Lisbon—the fact that Manuel had asked her to marry him.

In an uneasy political climate where dark clouds had started to gather, Manuel and Gaby made hay while the sun was still shining. There were walks in the country and cozy, candlelit suppers in front of the log fire. Out in the garden, under their window, the king's *guitarradas* played folk-songs and sang *fados*. Guards were stationed at each entrance of the Palais de Las Neccessitades, and when Manuel asked Gaby if she would like a companion to ease the boredom of the long hours when he had to return to the palace to fulfil his royal duties, she asked for José-Maria Lavradio.

In a government which day by day was becoming increasingly

more corrupt—ruled not by a king, but by his tyrannical mother—it may be that Lavradio was the only person that Manuel trusted. And if the price of this trust was Gaby Deslys on what would appear to have been a time-share basis, the king was in no position to complain.

It was Lavradio, and not Manuel, who was responsible for the sudden and dramatic change in Gaby's character. One afternoon when the king could not get away from the palace he asked Gaby's stand-in lover to take her on an outing. Both donned disguises and set off on foot but instead of escorting her into the centre of Lisbon he took her to the suburb of Alcantara, then as now one of the poorer but more colourful districts of the city. Gaby was appalled by the squalor and poverty here. Opening her purse she doled out all the money she had on her person to some of the children, and promised to return in the near future to do all she could to help alleviate the misery and suffering that, Lavradio informed her, the Portuguese government had always chosen to ignore. To cheer her up after what she had seen, he next took her to the botanical gardens, where she asked him to teach her the names of all the flowers in Portuguese. Her intention, she said, was to repeat them to one of her songwriters when she returned to Paris, and that a song would come about in honour of the country she now loved as much as her own. She still naively believed that Manuel would marry her and that she would be proclaimed Queen of Portugal—that even then, despite her royal status, she would still commute regularly between Paris and Lisbon and continue with her career.

When Gaby left Lisbon a few days later, she left behind two broken hearts. José-Maria Lavradio had merely given her his body and his love—Manuel both, along with a diamond-studded collar worth a million francs. What she had given them to remember her by, for now, was typical: a scented envelope containing clippings of her pubic hair.

After a brief rest at Number Three, Gaby travelled to Berlin. Her friend Will Bishop had asked her to play a short season at the Metropol, though what she did here is not known. She set tongues wagging by dining publicly with Crown Prince Wilhelm, an unpopular man with a reputation for lechery. From Berlin she headed for London, where on 28 March 1910 she opened at the Alhambra with *Les Caprices de Suzette*, a near-copy of some of the revues that Mistinguett had been putting on in Paris for over a decade. The British public in general were not to know this, and the revue was a massive success. It had just closed when, on 10 May, England was plunged into the deepest mourning with the death of Edward VII. The king had done much to promote the music-hall on both sides of the Channel. Gaby stayed on in London until after the funeral, though she was requested not to attend it and risk turning a sombre occasion into a circus.

At the end of May, Manuel contacted Gaby and invited her to Lisbon. José-Maria Lavradio had told him about their visit to Alcantara, and of how she had been moved by the plight of the district's poor people. Without hesitation, she agreed to appear in a revue and donate her entire salary towards helping them. Her entourage and most of her friends were delighted that, for the first time, she was doing something for others. Madame Paravicini tried to talk her out of it. Not only did she disapprove of Gaby's relationship with Manuel, she told her that, two years after the assassination of King Carlos, the country was again on the verge of revolt. For a little while, the agent was convinced that her charge had taken her advice. Gaby fell victim to an attack of influenza which laid her low for several weeks, and was unaware that a number of Portuguese papers had been delivered to the French Press Agency. These revealed that her affair with Manuel was now out in the open, and had been publicly condemned by Queen Amália.

Shortly before leaving for Portugal, Gaby visited Paul Poiret's studio. She planned wearing the gown he had designed for *Sans rancune* in Lisbon and, handing over a diamond-studded collar given to her by Manuel, she asked him to embellish this with "the four rarest bird of paradise feathers in the world", and commissioned a gold-lamé turban to match. Poiret told her that such a task would be simplicity itself, to which Gaby responded that this was just as well—she needed it for the next day!

On 12 July, Manuel left Lisbon for his father's hunting lodge in Bussaco Forest Park, near the university town of Coimbra. Gaby had taken the train to the Spanish border two days previously, but instead of travelling all the way to the Portuguese capital, as per her lover's instructions she got off at Villa Formosa. A car was waiting to drive her the sixty or so miles to the hunting lodge, formerly a convent, set in 100 acres of woodland. Here, the couple planned to stay until—or so Manuel hoped—Queen Amália, yet to find him a suitable bride, had come to her senses and realized just how much her son loved this "promiscuous showgirl". Events did not, however, work out the way they had planned. On 15 August, a piece appeared in *O Mundo*, and the writer did not mince his words:

> Public opinion is offended by the presence of the "théâtreuse" Gaby Deslys in Bussaco. We believe that it is an unpardonable sin to see this Parisian trollop frolicking in what was once a religious place where people came to do penance… This scandal has received much condemnation. A wealthy marquise who attends the royal court has petitioned the government to take a stand on this matter.

That same week, *Illustracao Portuguesa* published a photograph of Princess Patricia of Connaught, announcing that she and Manuel were soon to be married. They now ran an advertisement for Martial & Armand in which Gaby was wearing the Parisian fashion house's latest creation—a feathered hat and embroidered gown which, the caption said, was perfect enough to please even a king. The piece could not have appeared at a worse time. The Socialist government had been unstable for some time, with the rival Republican Party increasing in power and a revolution seeming likely. On 28 August, the legislative elections took place, resulting in a divided assembly which helped the revolutionaries: 58% Government, 33% Opposition and 9% Republican.

Manuel meanwhile travelled back to Lisbon, taking Gaby with him. She was most likely installed again at the Palais de Las Neccessitades though some reports suggested that she had actually been smuggled into the royal palace itself. Refusing to believe that she might have been in any danger, she was insistent that her charity event for the poor of Alcantara should still take place. Manuel begged her to cancel, at least until the political situation had settled, but she refused to listen. The starving people were of more importance, she declared, than "a few soldiers with swords".

When Gaby walked on to the stage of the Teatro Nacional de São Carlos—the scene of her earlier triumph—wearing the dress and hat that she had worn in the photograph in *Illustracao Portuguesa*—she was greeted with a tirade of hisses and boos. She glanced up anxiously at the royal box, hoping for encouragement from Manuel, but he was not there—his mother, anticipating trouble, had locked him in his room. Even so, Gaby nodded for the musicians to strike up the introduction to her first song, "La Parisienne", under the circumstances not a wise choice. Even worse was the one which followed. Most of them only recognized the melody of "Amor sou tua", while the ones in the audience who understood French soon "clicked" that the Antonio in the song—

the regal man who gave his love a carnation, was in reality their king! Some of those sitting in the stalls in front of the stage clambered over the orchestra to get at her. Some actually drew weapons, though no shots were fired. Gaby fled the stage and locked herself in her dressing-room. Curiously, the police were not summoned—just a disguised José-Maria Lavradio, who arrived with a small army of friends who managed to fight their way through the crush and rescue Gaby. She was given time to change out of her costume and into the dress she had arrived at the theatre in, and secreted out of the theatre via a side-entrance. From here, Lavradio drove her to the railway station, where an angry mob of anti-royalists were gathered outside the entrance. When one of these screamed in French that they were going to lynch her, Gaby realized that this was no bluff. Lavradio drove her to a station on the outskirts of the city, the furthest he dared venture away from the palace without arousing suspicion. She spent the entire night sitting on the platform, and during the journey to the Spanish border hid in the baggage compartment.

Gaby was met at the Gare d'Austerlitz by her mother, and a barrage of reporters. Most of these were able to see the lighter side of her affair with Manuel, and were interested only in the much-worshipped star and what her next theatrical venture was going to be—and not interested in criticising the "cold-hearted seductress" denounced by the Portuguese press. One journalist observed, "Gaby Deslys is a new national heroine, a Joan of Arc reborn on the banks of the Tagus!"

During the run of *Sans rancune*, Gaby's prospects of touring the United States had been discussed at length. She did not have a full-time agent, preferring to supervise all her own bookings, advised by Madame Paravicini whom she had kept on a retainer. She distrusted agents, she said, and in any case the commission they would have demanded was better in her pocket than in theirs, or rather set aside in her bank account ready to be handed over to the poor of Alcantara when she returned to Portugal, which she was hoping to do once the political situation there settled.

That summer she had been approached by André Charlot (1882-1956), an associate of Alfred Moul who managed several Parisian theatres, including the Folies-Bergère. Another interested associate was the German-born American showman H. B. Marinelli (1864-1924), who had co-directed her in *Au music-hall* at the Olympia in 1905 and who had offices in Paris, London and New York. A former contortionist who worked under the name, "The Boneless Wonder", he had stopped performing in 1898. Besides booking artistes as diverse as George Robey, Sir Harry Lauder and La Belle Otéro, Marinelli had earlier in the year organized Polaire's trip across the Atlantic. As part of the publicity campaign, a substantial reward had been promised to any American woman "of a certain age" willing to step forward and reveal a waistline smaller than Polaire's legendary 18-inch one. By the end of the tour she had claimed the reward for herself—and used this to buy a young black "slave" named Jimmy.

In her memoirs, Polaire claimed that Jimmy was only fourteen, but he was sixteen, and he stayed with her for many years. Neither did she care when accused of "cohabiting" with a minor, because unless someone saw them in the act, there was no proof that they were having sex. He was, she said her latest pet and to prove a point she bought him a silver medallion, inscribed, "J'appartiens à Polaire. Revenir, s'il vous plait, si trouvé" (I belong to Polaire. Please return if found). H. B. Marinelli was aware of Gaby's infatuation with Polaire, and tried to persuade the older star to visit Number Three and talk Gaby into signing up for a season in New York. Polaire still wanted nothing to do with her, but sent a message via Jimmy. Despite the instruction engraved on his medallion, Gaby did not return him at once to his owner. She kept him for the night, according to Régine Flory, "to teach him how real Frenchwomen fucked." In the future, whenever she fancied "something different", she would borrow Jimmy. And her answer was the same as she had told Marinelli once before. She was not ready to brave a week-long sea journey when her last Channel crossing had left her feeling ill for days afterwards.

Gaby *did* accept Marinelli's revue at the Folies-Bergère, and rehearsals began during the second week of September, when he and André Charlot joined forces in liaising with Jake and Lee Shubert, in New York—their aim to make Gaby an offer she would have been "insane" to refuse, mindless of her terror of the sea. Along with Florenz Ziegfeld, the Shubert brothers ruled the vaudeville scene in New York, and though Gaby's fee was not revealed, they are known to have offered her as much for ten appearances on Broadway as she had earned for the 100-plus performances of *Sans rancune. Still* she turned them down, her excuse now being that she needed to be within travelling distance of Lisbon, should Manuel need her. Then at the last minute the Folies-Bergère revue had to be cancelled, for just days ahead of the premiere, Gaby caught a chill and lost her voice. La Belle Otéro, as renowned for her "gastronomical desires"—in other words, gluttony—as Gaby was for her boudoir antics, was brought in to replace her at the eleventh hour.

At the end of September, Gaby headed for Vienna, where she opened at the Apollo Theatre in a "slightly abridged" version of *Les Caprices de Suzette*—amended to the effect that, though she would be thrilling audiences with her dancing and mimicry, they would not hear her singing unless she felt well enough to do so. Here, there was an adventure which she could well have done without, when a shabbily-dressed woman, who gave her name as Madame Navratil, barged into her dressing-room after the show and announced that *she* and not Anna Caire was her real mother!

Gaby sent her away, but Madame Navratil returned to the theatre each evening for a week before being carted off by the police. And if Gaby was hoping to have seen the last of her, she would be in for a shock.

While this drama was playing out, Gaby was unaware of what was happening in Portugal. On 4 October, violence erupted in the streets of Lisbon. Anticipating this, Manuel had retreated to the Palais de Las Neccessitades, but when this was bombarded by revolutionaries he escaped to the Mafra National Palace, where he was joined by Queen Amália and his grandmother, Maria Pia of Savoy. In and around the city there were scuffles, but Manuel's Loyalist supporters managed to keep these under control. At around eleven, he retired to his room, assured by his mother that the revolution would be short-lived once the populace had been convinced that he had amended his "philandering" ways. Hours later, he was awakened by the clamour of canons being fired in the harbour. His brief reign was over. An unruly crowd surged into the palace grounds and began chanting anti-royalist slogans beneath his window. Manuel instructed one of his ministers to summon the army, to be told that it had been commandeered by Antonio Machado, the Republican leader. When he attempted to address these insurgents, a grenade was thrown at him—he kicked this off the balcony, and it missed the crowd and exploded against the palace wall. Attempting to flee from the palace, he ran into the Republican guards. Though he yielded without a fight, he was beaten up and bundled into the back of a car, and driven the twenty miles north-west of the city to the palace at Sintra. A few hours later he was joined by Queen Amália, Maria Pia of Savoy, and a dozen or so retainers.

Antonio Machado issued a press statement, declaring that the revolution had been an unprecedented success, without so much as one drop of blood being spilled. This was untrue. Many palace guards were murdered by the Republicans, eager to filch the royal treasures. Anything too heavy to carry far was taken outside and burned, including priceless works of art and Manuel's unique collection of antique furniture. The insurgents also besieged convents known to have sheltered Loyalist adherents, raping and butchering nuns. The death-toll after the two-day bloodbath was estimated at 3,000, many of these innocent bystanders.

On the morning of 6 October, the royal captives were taken to Ericeira, a fishing port 22-miles northwest of Lisbon, and installed at a convent from where Manuel cabled the Portuguese embassy in London, and asked for asylum. As he was supposed to be marrying an English princess this was granted, and the next morning he and his company boarded the royal yacht, *Amália IV*. What happened next is unclear. The likeliest scenario is that the captain found out once they were at sea that he and his crew would not be allowed into England, and headed for the nearest port, Gibraltar—where he unceremoniously dumped his royal cargo before returning to Portugal to face the music. From here, Manuel cabled London and was told to stay put until Edward VII's former yacht, the *Victoria and Albert*, was sent to collect them. They arrived in Portsmouth on 9 October.

For several days, the exiled royals lodged in London before moving to Wood Norton, near Evesham in Worcestershire. This was the seat of Amália's brother, the Duc d'Orleans, but so far as Manuel was concerned little more than a prison. Built after the fall of the French monarchy, the house was in the middle of a dense forest and surrounded by a ten-foot, spiked galvanized steel wall. Despite their plight, Amália had lost none of her fighting spirit, and Manuel was still under her thumb. No sooner had they settled in than she resumed her quest to get him married.

The Deslys-Manuel affair appeared on the front pages of the world's press for several weeks. In Portugal, Manuel was defamed for giving her jewels and other costly gifts when his country had been on the verge of bankruptcy. Hoping to prevent some of these reports from getting out of hand, Gaby issued one statement after another. Not forgetting to blow her own trumpet, she told a Viennese reporter that Manuel's gifts to her were no more than the average bourgeois might give to the woman in his life—and in any case, *she* was probably wealthier than he was, now that he was no longer king. She gave a brief statement to Reuters when it was suggested that she might give up the stage in the wake of the scandal, but insisted this be published in the third person:

> Gabrielle Deslys has no desire to descend from the throne that she occupies today. She is a queen in the great work of art, whereas Portugal is but a petty state!

Though distressed by Manuel's deposition, Gaby was relieved that he had emerged from his ordeal with no more than a black eye and bruised ribs. She perceived the Portuguese revolution as a blessing in disguise—for as a "free" man, she believed that he would be able to shrug off his mother's influence and marry the woman he truly loved, instead of someone chosen for him. In England, *The Tatler* took her to task for her "conceited" comments:

> Mlle Deslys calls herself a Queen of the World of Art but in her case it is certainly a teeny-weeny little world. She is quite pretty of course, and she dances neatly, and the little upward curve of her mouth, so assiduously cultivated, is very fetching for a short time. But to turn her nose up at a real kingdom merely because one has a certain celebrity in the music-hall world is surely the very height of ridiculous feminine vanity, to which an equally

ridiculous public can encourage one of its pretty favourites.

In Vienna *Les Caprices de Suzette* continued to play to packed houses, and the director of the Apollo Theatre took advantage of this by increasing ticket prices—and, of course, Gaby's fee. She also paid her only visit to a recording studio. During her last season in London she had been approached by C. B. Smith of The Gramophone & Typewriter Company to cut two unspecified sides. She had refused, her excuse being that she was primarily a visual artiste and not a *chanteuse*. When he read a Reuter's report that Gaby had recovered her voice and she was in finer fettle than ever, Smith cabled his representative in Vienna, and she was offered £150—a phenomenal sum—to cut a minimum of eight songs which over the coming year would be issued on four 78 rpm records. The session took place during the afternoon of 15 October, but only five songs were laid down: *La Parisienne*, and two versions each of *Tout en rose* and *Philoméne*. She should have returned to the studio two days later, but did not.

The quality of these primitive recordings, which were discovered many years after Gaby's death by EMI London researcher Ruth Edge and myself, is astonishing, and her singing voice came as a very nice surprise. Ruth observed:

> I think you'll agree that her voice is very pleasing, though what I would call typically French. At times, it sounds as if she had no training, but now and then, on certain notes, there is more than a suggestion that she had singing lessons. Also her diction is very clear and precise.

Gaby's voice was in fact almost operatic, and her ability to switch from buffoonery to drama makes her a precursor of Europe's two greatest *fantaisistes*, Marie Dubas and Gracie Fields, though her strong Marseille accent is difficult to grasp. What is sad are the deep, sometimes choking gasps between some of the top notes—Gaby was already in poor health, unable to breathe properly, and her condition would only get worse.

Philoméne was a semi-comic number written for Gaby by Henri Christiné, who had just begun an important songwriting partnership with Vincent Scotto. Mistinguett, Polaire, Maurice Chevalier and Joséphine Baker all performed their work with great success. Scotto also composed *La Parisienne* (not to be confused with the earlier *Je chante la gloire de la Parisienne*) and perhaps the best of the trio, *Tout en rose*, which may almost be regarded as a precursor to Edith Piaf's later *La vie en rose*. Even so it is a peculiar number. It opens not with the verse but with the chorus, "Quand on aime, on voit toute en rose!" (When one loves, one sees everything in pink!), after which we hear only part of the verse before Gaby pronounces, in English, "To be or not to be, that is the question!" Then the melody and key changes completely, as if she has turned over two pages of music by mistake and begun another song entirely…ending with her telling the recording engineer, the Budapest Gramophone Company's Franz Hampe, "Naughty, naughty boy!" It would also appear that English and Portuguese lyrics were written for *Tout en rose*, to be recorded at a later date—the song does sound in parts a little like the folk song *O Tirana*, which Manuel had taught Gaby.

Les Caprices de Suzette closed during the last week of October 1910, when Gaby headed for Monte Carlo. She rested here for several weeks—celebrating her 29th birthday on 4 November before travelling to England, anxious to see Manuel. In the midst of the chaos of the past month she had contacted Mariano Unzué, who had sailed at once from Buenos Aires to be by her side. Cynics might have observed that if one of her men, Manuel, *was* planning on getting married, then at least she would have another waiting in the wings. When she arrived in London, accompanied by her mother, Mariano was waiting at the house he had rented for them in Knightsbridge.

There was no revue this time, just a number of personal appearances at hospitals and children's homes, for where charitable deeds were concerned Gaby really had turned over a new leaf. Mariano accompanied her everywhere, which must have been confusing for the reporters who trailed after her like camp followers. When asked about Manuel, she held nothing back regarding how much she loved him, and this angered her Argentinian escort—more than once when they met, Mariano and the ex-king almost came to blows. The situation grew so volatile that Anna Caire asked Mariano to leave the house which *he* was paying for! She then told Manuel that if he wanted to see Gaby, it would have to be under the eagle eye of a chaperone—herself. Ultimately, tragedy ensued. Gaby became so depressed that she took an overdose of sleeping pills. Anna Caire, anxious that this should not be made public, revealed how utterly two-faced she was by summoning Mariano. A doctor was called, who administered an emetic—then promptly sold the story to a newspaper. The suicide bid was virulently denied by Gaby, while Mariano decided that the only way to get her over her obsession with Manuel was to put some distance between them for a while. As soon as she was well enough to travel, he took her back to Paris, but not before she had signed a contract with Alfred Moul to appear in a season at the Alhambra, scheduled to take place during the spring or summer of 1911.

Within days of arriving back at Number Three, Gaby received a telegram from Florenz Ziegfeld, in New York. This proposed a three-months' tour of America, for which she would be paid $1,000 a week, four times the amount she would be getting for the

Alhambra. Gaby contacted Moul, and informed him that she would be going to America after all—and that if push came to shove, she would pay *him* what he was paying her, to get out of the Alhambra contract. Then just as quickly, she changed her mind. One month later, she opened at the Théâtre des Capucines in *Le Midi Bouge*, a three-part revue which saw her closing the show in a 25-minute sketch entitled *Les Débuts de Chichine*. The scenario for this was her own idea. Laid low with a chill, she had learned her lines in bed and decided that her boudoir should be replicated on the stage, with the director of the Capucines and Alfred Moul sharing the expenditure. Charles Bernel, the antiques dealer who supplied most of the furniture at her home, provided the theatre with original 18th century paintings, chandeliers, and a copy of Marie Antoinette's bed currently on display at the Palace of Versailles. This alone cost over £1,000, with the bill for the setting amounting to £3,500!

The sketch raised few eyebrows when presented to Gaby's more open-minded French public. When it premiered at the London Alhambra on 29 May 1911, it formed part of a triple bill, *The Dance Dream*, honouring the coronation of King George V, scheduled to take place on 22 June. Opening the show was Queenie Hall, with her *Mad Pierrot* mime act. Headlining were the Moscow Imperial Theatre Ballet's Vasily Tichomirov and Catrina Geltzer. The only time a bed had appeared on a London stage had been for someone to die in, and though Gaby's sketch was a comic one which today would seem tame, it was considered lewd by religious groups and moralists. Many of these picketed the theatre, which of course resulted in her playing to packed audiences and the three-weeks run extended to three months.

The storyline of this Feydeau-esque sketch was tells of Chichine the *coquette* with *three* lovers, each of whom proposes marriage. She decides that the lucky man will be he who succeeds in getting her on the stage, and she lounges in her boudoir while waiting for this to happen. When her nerves get the better of her, she grabs a gun—using real bullets and terrifying audiences—and shoots the cuckoo clock! René (Vermandéle), the singer in the apartment below, hears this and thinking she has shot herself, rushes into her room and gives her an impromptu singing lesson. They perform a duet and when he leaves Chichine sees Flip (Edgar Chatel) sitting in the fireplace. He has climbed down the chimney to give her a dancing lesson. They execute a high-kicking routine, after which Flip pretends to leave, hiding behind the curtains. Her last lover to arrive is Durton (Alfred Lugg), who tells her that he has secured her an engagement on the stage, though she thinks this is a trick. Then Flip reveals himself, René bursts into the room, and there is a brawl—followed by a song and dance routine which ends with Chichine and Durton rushing off, leaving the spurned lovers to console each other!

The critics were scathing, though Francis Tove defended Gaby in an unusually long article, "Fleur Deslys", At Whose Feet Respectability Worships!" in the 26 July edition *The Bystander*:

> Gaby Deslys delights me. I write this without a blush, almost with a sense of conscious virtue. I have abandoned an open admiration of Shaw, Wells and Galsworthy in favour of a "sneaking delight" in the under-garments of Mlle Deslys. I have tasted the joys of an unhoped-for respectability. Of course, we are not interested in the artiste, the person who dances indifferently, and sings rather well. All our admiration goes to the woman. And Gaby, bless her heart, knows this as well as we do. All we ask of Mlle Deslys is to make Chichine as much like herself as possible. We do not even care about the three lovers…the "coquette" is the important thing. What more

can any honest man want? She is the symbol of Paris as the ordinary Englishman imagines it…extraordinarily attractive, with her attractiveness coming mainly from the advertisement of her femininity. Everything about her is exaggerated, from her rouge and powder to her flimsy garments. She triumphs, turning men round her finger like wisps of straw, teasing them, petting them…working her wicked way on them in a thousand ways. All this is very flattering on the vanity of the sex, though in practice many women, I am thankful to say, would shrink from doing any such thing. But oh, we English are wonderful people, particularly those of us who happen to be respectable!

During this visit to London, Gaby stayed at the Savoy, with the tab picked up by Alfred Moul. Though Mariano escorted her almost everywhere during the daytime, and back and forth to the theatre, he had no idea what she was getting up to once he dropped her back at the hotel after the show. The manager took exception to the number of male visitors she was getting, and ordered her to leave. Jacques-Charles, in London at the time, attempted to defend her reputation but only made matters worse by observing in his memoirs that she was *politely* requested to leave because she had developed a fever—and that the manager had not wished for her to pass on whichever infectious disease she had to his other clients! Jacques-Charles adds that he, and not Mariano, found her a small flat nearby, and that he subsequently acted as third party when arranging for her to meet Manuel after her mother had gone to bed. He concludes that such was her gratitude that, should he ever find himself in a fix, she promised to return the favour.

The revue closed. Gaby, her mother and Mariano returned to Paris where one afternoon a surprise visitor turned up at Number

Three—Jake Shubert, in the middle of a talent-spotting trip to Europe, offered her a tour of the United States, on her own terms. What Shubert did not add was that the Americans were far less interested in whether she could actually *do* anything than they were in seeing the scandalous woman who had cost a king his throne. Gaby reeled off her terms. She would require a minimum $4,000 a week, first-class travelling expenses for herself and her entourage, and a generous allowance for costumes and sets. Three cyclists would have to be at her beck-and-call 24 hours a day to deal with the hundreds of messages and letters she anticipated sending and receiving while in America. She had also heard that the streets in New York were unclean—therefore a sedan chair would have to be provided to carry her from the hotel entrance to her carriage, and from here to her dressing-room! Shubert would also have to pay her $10,000 in advance. Additionally, her contract should contain a clause stating that if she wanted to return to London or Paris "for urgent personal reasons"—in other words, if summoned back by Manuel—she should be allowed to do so, thus nullifying her contract. Shubert stunned her by agreeing, adding a few generous conditions of his own, not least of all that such a contract would be for three extensive tours over a three-year period. Then, hoping to ensure that she did *not* throw in the towel on account of a whim, he agreed to increase her weekly salary by $1,000 for each year she continued working for him.

Mariano made arrangements for Gaby to travel to New York. Her first revue would include *Les Débuts de Chichine*, and before Jake Shubert left Paris she told him that she would be unable to perform in this unless the props—including the mock-Marie Antoinette bed, in storage in London—accompanied her across the ocean! Shubert agreed. She then dropped the bombshell that Mariano and her mother would *not* be accompanying her, for this was one gamble she would make standing on her own feet. Neither was she worried about the venture being a success. The terms of her contract ensured her that even if the trip was a failure, she would return home one of the wealthiest women in France. In short, she had nothing to lose. What she had no idea of knowing was that, after America, her life would never be the same again—for in New York she would meet a man who would give a whole new meaning to the word "love".

Les débuts de Chichine.

Manuel II of Portugal, pictured at the time he and Gaby became lovers.

Manuel and Lavradio, London, 1909.

Polaire with Jimmy, her 16-year-old "slave" lover who Gaby borrowed from time to time.

Les caprices de Suzette, a rare occasion when Gaby was photographed with a cigarette.

4: I'm Just Wild About Harry!

Early in 1919, Gaby Deslys would give a very frank interview to the French journalist, Michel-Georges Michel, in which America and the greatest love of her life would figure prominently:

> Everything was so *big* over there—and I do mean everything! All I had to do was pose for a few photographs. I helped them to sell their cars. And in any case, how could I refuse? I was earning upwards of twenty-two thousand francs a week. Six times a day, a millionaire asked me to marry him. I tried to bring a crocodile home, but it died while I was trying to get it through customs. And of course, I brought back a man!

This man was Harry Pilcer, and though predominantly gay, he would remain the great love of her life—more so than Manuel of Portugal—even when their ardour had cooled somewhat, until the end. Curiously, she would describe him in the past tense:

> Harry was of medium height, with a narrow waist and nice, tight buttocks. His shoulders were broad, his chest muscular. Like everything else in America, he was big where it mattered! In many ways he was an innocent child, yet I assure you he was a man through and through! His lips were the most sensual that I have ever kissed. Harry was the most beautiful, virile man I have ever known!

Innocent, Harry was not. He was born in New York on 29 April 1885. His Hungarian parents Samuel and Elsie had emigrated here a few years earlier, virtually penniless, but after a short while had founded a prosperous tailoring business in the Jewish quarter. After Harry there had been five more Pilcers, none of whom showed any interest in following in their father's footsteps. Louis, Joseph and Eddie went into business. Murray and Elsie, like Harry, made a living in the music-hall—the former as a drummer and bandleader, the latter in vaudeville.

At twelve, Harry began skipping school to take dancing lessons. Samuel Pilcer found out, but instead of rebuking him allowed him to have his way, convinced that in time he would tire of his "fad" and aspire towards a more worthwhile profession. Harry persisted, appearing in his first off-Broadway revue in 1899 as a chorus member. When he left school at fifteen, Samuel stopped his allowance and for two years he took on bit-parts and jobs working backstage to support himself. This paid poorly, and by seventeen he was supplementing his income by working as an escort, picking up clients in subway stations, restaurants and on street corners—never fussy about their gender so long as they paid up front. He had already developed the sexual potency, aided by his stunning physique and ethereal looks, which would in years to come compliment the magical effect of his dancing.

Early in 1906, Harry secured himself a place at the Claude Alviene School of Dance where a fellow student was Fred Astaire. This saw him becoming involved with Alviene's producer-choreographer partner, Ned Wayburn (1874-1942), who had just set up his own outfit, the Headline Vaudeville Production Company with which he liaised with other big name producers of the day including the Shuberts, Lew Fields, and later with Florenz Ziegfeld. After trying Harry out in numerous chorus lines, Wayburn gave him his first major part in *The Side Show* which previewed in February 1907 at New Jersey's Trenton Theatre, and transferred to Brooklyn's Hyde & Behman Theatre in April. Such a scenario—actors playing what the publicity sheet called "twenty suborninate people"—would not have been allowed today. *The Brooklyn Eagle* observed:

> It is one of the funniest vaudeville sketches that has come to Brooklyn. The freaks of the circus side-show are shown up, the members of the chorus assuming the various disguises in the presence of the audience…the dog-faced boy and the wild-man from Borneo are shown to be fakes, pure and simple. Harry Pilcer and little Dot Williams, who head the cast, are a clever pair and make a good background for the revel of the freaks. It was all so very amusing…

When the show moved to Springfield, Massachusetts, there were complaints about Harry's costumes. One sketch called for him to dance in a swimsuit which one newspaper denounced as "skimpy, revealing and ungodly". In effect, it revealed his legs from above the knee, much of his chest—and, horror of horrors, his unshaven armpits. After the premiere, the theatre manager ordered him to remove this "excessive" body hair, and to get a haircut before his next performance. Harry shaved his chest, but ignored the other demands and adding insult to injury oiled his upper half to enhance his muscular physique. One journalist was so incensed that he waited for Harry outside the stage door, levelled a few homophobic insults—and got a good deal more than he bargained for when the young man gave him a pasting. The next evening, two police officers were waiting in Harry's dressing-room. During the subsequent interrogation, he passed out. The theatre doctor who examined him declared that he had fainted "on account of divine intervention", and the journalist dropped the charge of assault.

The tour continued with mixed reviews, mostly condemning Harry for his "immorality", but praising him for his remarkably athletic routines. The real reason for his passing out in Springfield was because of a chest infection which grew worse as the tour progressed. In Waterbury, Connecticut, he collapsed in the wings and was rushed to a local hospital where doctors diagnosed double-bronchial pneumonia. He was transferred to a clinic in New York, and over the coming week his condition deteriorated to an extent that his parents were told to expect the worst. He recovered, returned to hustling, and embarked on a love affair with an unnamed theatre manager who secured him an audition with Jules Hurtig—with his partner Harry Seamon for a while almost on a par with the Shubert Brothers in vaudeville.

With Hurtig and Seamon, Harry signed a five-year contract, and his first appearance was to have been in a revue entitled *Young Sleuth*. For some reason, this was cancelled shortly after rehearsals began and, aided by his father who in the wake of *The Side Show*'s success had decided to support his career after all, he sued Hurtig and Seamon for $1,700. He was "rescued" by Charles E. Blaney of New York's Lincoln Square Theatre. Though married, Blaney (1866-1944) was as interested in the young man as he was in his dancing skills, and contracted him to appear in a pantomime. *The Bad Boy and His Teddy Bears* opened at the Lincoln Square Theatre on 23 December 1907, the week that Harry's case against Hurting and Seamon was heard at the Seventh Municipal Court. He won his case, but it was a pyrrhic victory when the judge slashed his $1,700 claim by half.

Harry's notices for the show were exceptional, primarily because he had been given freedom to choreograph not just his own sketches, but those for the entire production. He also sang two songs in the production—*When The Minstrels Come To Town* and, in a duet with Eileen Sheridan, *You Are Not The One For Me*.

The story was trite, but audiences loved it, as did the critic with *The New York Times*:

> A family of brown bears and the prankish lad who has made their acquaintance figure very prominently in the action, which opens at the Mountain View Health Resort. The proprietor has invented a rain-making machine, and he persuades a visiting railway magnate, Henry Harrington, to buy this. Harrington's son, Percy [Harry] then falls in love with the owner's daughter, Alice [Eileen Sheridan], and wants to wed her…only she doesn't care for him at all and wants to marry Jacques Floto, one of the summer boarders. Percy then becomes so disagreeable that Chips, one of Alice's friends, summons his Teddy Bears and they cart her off to their home in the forest…an underground domicile very much like Peter Pan's house. This is the most interesting feature of the piece, especially to juvenile audiences. After hiding with the bears for a while, Percy and his Alice go away, and return married, and the play ends with a scene entitled "A Society Circus", featuring some very clever dancing from Pilcer, especially the cakewalk.

The revue closed on 18 January 1908, and for over a year—on account of a recurrence of bronchial pneumonia—Harry only worked spasmodically. In the autumn, he moved into an apartment with a chorus boy. He was just twenty-three but sufficiently affluent to pick and choose his roles even if these did not pay well. His next part—unbilled but very important for his quickly progressing career—was dancing in the chorus of *Ziegfeld Follies*, which opened at the New York Theatre in June 1909. Hustling was an integral part of his psyche, nevertheless, not for money as his fame grew, but for the thrill of it, and he still "worked his beat" after the show. One of his clients was Al Jolson. They had a brief affair, the consequences of which would be far-reaching and potentially harmful towards both their careers, and which would come very close to destroying that of Gaby Deslys when she began working in America.

Whether Florenz Ziegfeld (1867-1932) became involved with Harry is not known, but not impossible. Born in Chicago, he was the son of a German immigrant who spent some time in Paris, acquainting himself with the music-hall there. He began staging his *Follies* in 1907, each replicating a Parisian setting typical of those featuring the likes of Gaby and Mistinguett. And while these ladies' revues employed the cream of the crop where French songwriters were concerned, Ziegfeld's production numbers were choreographed to the works of Jerome Kern, George Gershwin and Irving Berlin. With the exception of Nora Bayes, the headliners in *Follies of 1909* are forgotten today, but future *Follies* would boast some of the biggest names of the day: Fanny Brice, W. C. Fields, Eddie Cantor, Lilliane Lorraine, Ruth Etting—and Billie Burke and Anna Held, two of Ziegfeld's wives.

The show closed in August 1909, and Harry left New York for Chicago, where he successfully auditioned for the male lead in *The Flirting Princess*. Promoted as "A Nonsense Farce", this opened at the La Salle Theatre on 1 November 1909. He played the part of "Jack Stuart, apache and vampire dancer" whose big number was *There Are Too Many Girls in the World*. He raised a few titters, and more than a few eyebrows, when he performed, *Oh, Those Men!*—dressed as a woman. The critic with the *New York Dramatic Mirror* unpleasantly observed,

> Mr. Pilcer in woman's clothes. There are possibilities, as in a similar elastic production, but the fad for queer dances

now in the possession of the producer's mind is retarding development.

The Flirting Princess closed in April 1910 after 240 performances and Harry returned to New York to spend time with his parents. While here he was contacted by Florenz Ziegfeld. The showman had read the notices for his revues, and urged him to stay in the city and work with Lillian Lorraine on a number of song-and-dance routines for the forthcoming *Ziegfeld Follies of 1910*. Ziegfeld had purloined Lorraine (1892-1955) from Jake Shubert in 1907 after seeing her in *The Tourists*, and she had become his mistress—even though she was only fifteen, and he could have been charged with statutory rape. The following year he had put her into his revue, *Miss Innocence*, where she had introduced her theme song, *By the Light of the Silvery Moon*. Volatile did not even begin to describe her. In the few years that she was applauded as "The Number One Ziegfeld Girl" she managed to fall out with just about everyone she worked with. The first person she crossed swords with during rehearsals was Fanny Brice, who was brought in to headline with Harry, when Lorraine believed that it should have been her. The next was Harry, who she took an instant dislike to—with Lorraine, there never had to be a reason. Never less than a law unto himself, Harry told Ziegfeld that he would stay with the revue only until he had found a replacement, and that after that he would be returning to Chicago. Ziegfeld pleaded with him to reconsider—well aware that having Brice and Pilcer on the same bill would guarantee HOUSE FULL notices being put up in the foyer every evening—and Harry appears to have given him reassurance that he *would* stay. Such was the stress of working with Lorraine that he went back on his word and accepted a part in another revue *before* the 20 June premiere—one which would open while *Follies of 1910* was in full-swing. He revealed this to the theatre critic with *The Chicago News,* who in turn broke the news in his review of the show before Harry got around to telling Ziegfeld that he was about to leave him in the lurch:

> Another Chicago contingent sweeps in and captures all the applause! Harry Pilcer came out of the West and set Flo's *Follies of 1910* upon dancing feet with tremendous dramatic consequence. There's no story only the usual shimmering string of specialities and choral jigs and high jinks…a freshet of stripped women, and willowy legs floundering and cavorting a rain of silken sheen and a general riot of diabolism and dance. Harry Pilcer and a handsome creature called Vera Maxwell, also from Chicago, do the most wonderfully brilliant dance seen on the stage for years and Pilcer, who is rather a foolish young person of great personal beauty, has hitherto passed his stage time in changing his clothes. He leaps on to the stage in a satin garb of orchid hues and does the Old Fandango Rag in a sensual and dazzling way. It is the hit of the piece, and Flo has offered Pilcer his own terms for next year…Harry, however, goes with Elsie Janis and leaves *The Follies* disconsolate!

The new revue was *The Slim Princess,* produced by Charles Dillingham—a rival of the Shuberts— scheduled to play a short season in Chicago before embarking on a national tour and culminating at New York's Globe Theatre in January 1911. Harry was to play Philadelphia millionaire Alex Pike, though he was not overtly pleased to learn who his leading lady was to be. The temperamental musical-comedy star Elsie Janis had never worked with him, though they had met once when she had made it only too obvious that she had been attracted him. Harry was not in the least interested in her. He had his chorus-boy back in Chicago—and Ned Wayburn, for now. Even so, he told Dillingham that he would "grin and bear it for the sake of his art".

Janis (Elsie Bierbower, 1889-1956) had headlined revues since the age of eleven. A gifted mimic and comedienne, she later added composer and script-writer to her roster of talents, besides being NBC Radio's first female presenter. The show premiered at Chicago's Studebaker Theatre on 18 September, and was a big hit—Harry and Janis's production number, *My Yankee Doodle Girl*, received a five-minutes standing ovation. The pair were all smiles when meeting journalists at the post-performance party, most of whom were unaware of their expletives-laden backstage fights. This became evident as the Chicago season progressed. Janis was unhappy with the storyline, that of a princess who comes from a land where obesity is the equivalent of being beautiful—hence the quotes in the press about Dillingham having fattened her up to make her look prettier than she really was, but that she made up for her ugliness with the sweetness of her singing! Harry on the other hand found himself placed upon a pedestal by James O'Donnell Bennett of *The Record Herald*:

> He is soft, sweet and familiarly epileptic. The personal beauty of Mr. Pilcer, when coupled with a howling dervish, is alive with the grace and fire of a Russian court dancer.

Percy Hammond of *The Chicago Daily Tribune*, sitting closer to the stage than his colleagues, was less enthusiastic:

> In one of his dances with Miss Janis, Mr. Pilcer leers, and he should not do this, for when he leers he looks like a cobra.

By the time *The Slim Princess* reached Philadelphia on 31 October Harry and Janis were no longer on speaking terms, and he refused to attend the press conference after the show. The next stop on the road was Pittsburgh, but on 24 November, four days before the premiere, Harry and Janis had one bust-up too many. He walked out of the production and returned to Chicago, and was replaced by Wallace McCutcheon, later briefly married to "Queen of the Serials" actress Pearl White.

Harry was next commissioned by Ned Wayburn to choreograph a sketch for Joe Howard's revue, *Love and Politics*, which opened at Chicago's Cort Theatre on 3 April 1911. He devised the *Frisco Frizz*, a frenzied routine which brought the house down. During another routine, he allowed himself to go too far. Ripping off the front of his shirt, he wrapped himself around a pillar and, according to one critic, "simulated the act of copulation". The curtain was brought down as some of those sitting in the stalls rushed the stage, causing Harry to flee to his dressing-room and lock the door. Incredibly, the performance was allowed to continue, and he returned to the stage at the end of the show to reprise the *Frisco Frizz*. The next morning the theatre manager, Sport Herman, summoned Harry to his office and informed him that the "vulgar" routine would have to be removed from his sketch. Harry refused. Many of the first night audience had walked out in disgust, but this had awarded the piece such notoriety that within hours of the ticket office opening, the entire season had sold out—many tickets purchased by Harry's speedily growing following of gay admirers. Even so, Herman told Harry that unless he cleaned up his act, he would be fired. Harry ignored this, and after the next matinee performance he was escorted off the stage by two security men and taken to Herman's office. When the trio set upon him, he defended himself this time not with his fists, but with a heavy electric fan—hitting the security men with this before flinging it at Herman. During the scuffle, he tripped over a wire and banged his face on the desk. The next morning, the *Chicago Telegraph* twisted the story around to Herman's advantage—*Harry* had come off worst, and been taken by cab to his hotel room, "battered beyond immediate availability".

The Cort Theatre debacle did Harry's career no harm—quite the opposite, for on account of the scandal the offers came pouring in. He was offered a contract by Jake Shubert, who wanted him to star in *The Revue of Revues*, set to open at the New York Winter Garden on 27 September. Harry turned Shubert down, not just because he received a better offer from Ned Wayburn to perform his *Frisco Frizz* routine in *Hello Paris*, at New York's Folies-Bergère, but because he would be expected to share the bill with a woman who, where America was concerned, was yet to prove herself possessed of any singular talent other than that of bringing down a monarchy…Gaby Deslys.

"I am not having that tart stealing my thunder," he is quoted as having told Shubert.

How things would soon change!

Harry Pilcer, aged 20.

The playbill for *The Bad Boy & His Teddy Bears*.

5: When Two Worlds Collide

Gaby's crossing to New York was not an easy one. During the first few days of the voyage she suffered terribly as the *Lorraine* was tossed and battered by storms. Only the thought of the money she would be earning once she reached New York kept her spirits up—and the fun she had once she had recovered from her indisposition. Her fellow passengers expected her to be outrageous, and she did not disappoint, entertaining a succession of sailors, toffs and "lowly" cabin boys in her luxurious stateroom.

On 17 September 1911, several hours before the boat docked, the news of Gaby's imminent arrival was wired to reporters gathered in front of the customs-house. These were in for a long wait—the harbour was blanketed in thick fog, though this only added to the air of excitement when she materialised from this on the gangway, wearing an arctic-fox coat, which she opened to reveal the pearls given to her by Manuel of Portugal. The last ten years of her life had been spent bathing in publicity, so this was nothing new. For several minutes, without saying a word, she posed for photographs.

Gaby's official escort was Fred Wright, who had partnered her three years previously in *Son Altesse l'Amour*, at the Moulin-Rouge. Wright was currently appearing at the New Amsterdam Theatre in *The Pink Lady*. He had organised for porters to convey her thirty trunks into the customs-house. Supervised by two private detectives hired by Jake Shubert, these were opened and checked by officials, who estimated her jewels alone to be worth over $320,000—by today's standards, around $4 million! Wright then escorted her to the car provided to drive her to the St Regis Hotel, and when she tried to tip the driver he informed her that the vehicle was hers! Outside the hotel, admirers who had seen only pictures of her in the newspapers showered her with confetti and rose-petals. When asked if she was surprised by her ecstatic reception she pronounced, in broken English, "But of course not. I *am* the biggest star in France!" In the foyer, she reluctantly consented to a press-conference, and was soon wishing she had not. The reporters were interested only in how much her pearls were worth, if her hair was *naturally* blonde—and the Manuel affair. Initially she pretended not to understand questions she did not wish to answer, but soon lost her cool and asked Fred Wright to escort her up to her suite. Some of these reporters would reward her arrogance by slating her performances, whether they were good or not.

Gaby resented the fact that the Shubert brothers had changed their minds about staging *Les Débuts de Chichine* on Broadway, and instead put her into *The Revue of Revues.* She hit the roof when told that America's most famous dancer, Harry Pilcer, had refused to work with her—that instead of headlining her show, she would be *sharing* the bill with Frank Tinney, who she had never heard of—along with Harry Jolson, Al's older brother. There were more fireworks when Shubert informed her that a nation-wide tour would precede the 27 September premiere at the Winter Garden. Gaby Deslys was of such importance in France, she informed him, *not* to warrant try-outs in provincial theatres—adding that, as per her contract, she considered such downgrading of her talent an urgent personal reason to book herself on the next boat to France. Shubert had no alternative but to give in *and* to include *Les Débuts de Chichine* in the new show. The public may have been thrilled to see her playing a hilarious bedroom farce, but the critics were not. Most of them were of the opinion that she was not worth the $4,000 a week the Shuberts were paying her. Alan Dale, one of the reporters she snubbed in New York harbour and who would prove a constant thorn in her side, observed in *Variety*:

> It may be considered *au fait* for Frenchmen to make love in the bedchamber of their adored while she is attired in a short night-robe, but America does not believe in the system.

Harry had opened in *Hello Paris* on 19 August. On 27 September —three days before his show closed and on the day hers opened— Gaby attended a matinee performance at the Folies-Bergère to see what the fuss was about regarding the man who declared himself *above* working with her. Had it not been for Pilcer, she told reporters, *she* would have been playing *demimondaine* Fifi instead of Minerva Coverdale, who not only danced with this man but imitated *her*, with a Bronx-twanged French accent! If this was not enough, there was a sketch mocking her friend Liane de Pougy, in which Edith Rose portrayed her as "Liani de Pansy"! Gaby fell for Harry in a big way, especially when he tore off his shirt and wrapped himself around the pillar during the *Frisco Frizz*. She made up her mind there and then, whether she hated him or not, that she would have him. For now, he was not interested in anyone but his chorus-boy lover, who had followed him to New York and was living at his off-Broadway apartment.

Gaby was incensed by Alan Dale's championing of Harry while making it clear that he disliked her. To a man, the Chicago press had denounced the *Frisco Frizz*—now cynically re-baptized the *Pilcer Fuck*, on account of the way he mock-copulated with the pillar during the routine. Though Dale was not keen on the revue, he certainly appreciated Harry:

> An expurgated dance from a Chicago show was the one real live moment in 65 minutes of drear and drivel in the new "Midnight Revue" on Monday night. Mr. Pilcer did the dance then, when the police told him to stop. There is

also the *apache-vampire*, and though it will be an awfully nerve-wearing task to sit through the first sixty minutes to wait for this, it's worth the waiting for! Miss Coverdale is thinner than ever this season, for reasons that were apparent before she had half-finished the contortion stunt with her youthful partner. There was a touch of the Salome, the snake and muscle-dance in the pair's gyrations, who whirled about the stage like dervishes before tumbling down a flight of steps with all the abandon of foot-ballists. Pilcer varied his antics with a series of unexpected near back-handsprings and all the time seemed to be engaged in a mad effort to break Miss Coverdale's back.

Halfway through the run of *The Revue of Revues*, Jake Shubert removed Gaby from the show after complaints from his backers that she was not worth the inflated salary she was getting—and unworthy of the headline splashed across the billboards, "Gaby Deslys—The Most Fascinating Sensation Of All Europe". Neither did she do herself any favours when a journalist with the *New York Herald*, who interviewed her in French in her dressing-room, audaciously boasted that while Jake Shubert was paying her $4,000 a week, a revue artiste working at the Paris Opéra who was every bit as good as she was, if not better, was only getting the equivalent of $200 a week:

> I know that men have more respect for my jewels and for my beauty than for my talent. As long as I own my own house, my car and my pearls, I can hold the head high. The whole world can go to hell!

Jake Shubert believed Gaby *was* worth every cent he was paying her. He had a new revue coming up, *Vera Violetta*, set to open at the Winter Garden Theatre on 20 November. Its flimsy storyline recounted the amorous adventures of Adele de St-Cloche, the flirty wife of a stuffy professor. Vera Violetta was the name of her favourite Roger & Gallet perfume, and the waltz commissioned to celebrate it. With a libretto by Louis Stein and music by George M. Cohan and Edmund Eysler, and with additional material by Louis A. Hirsch and Jean Schwartz it was more of an operetta than a revue, though by the time the Shuberts and their tetchy stars had finished with it, it became little more than a contest of egos. The brothers hoped to team her with Harry, providing they could persuade *him* to appear not just with her, but with Al Jolson, who would also be in the show.

Jolson was terrified of Harry revealing that he had once paid him for sex. Yet despite this, and as if nurturing a career death-wish he had not stopped mocking him since. Jolson's dresser was a flagrantly homosexual man named Holmes, invariably introduced by the singer to all and sundry as "Pansy" Holmes. Jolson also took risks, certainly where the Shuberts were concerned, by including a sketch in his act where there was a fictional exchange between two effeminate Shubert chorus boys. Mincing across the stage, limp-wristed and with his bottom sticking out, he has one asking, "Do you know Nancy O'Neill?"—bringing the response from the other, "No. Who is he?" Jolson also hated Gaby. Though they had never met, he had heard enough about her from his brother, Harry, for him not to wish to work with her. Josie Collins, the British-born star whose mother Lottie's signature tune "Ta-Ra-Ra-Boom-Der-E" had been adapted for Polaire, and whose name would be heading the credits, initially resented Gaby because Gaby was earning four times as much as she was, though they later became good friends.

Jake Shubert knew that he had a massive problem on his hands which he believed would be easier solved if Gaby was not around while he was trying to mend bridges between Harry and Jolson. Thus she was sent on what should have been a six-venue tour with *The Gaby Deslys Vera Violetta Revue*, nothing to do with the revue he was planning, but a mish-mash of some of the songs she had performed in Paris, along with *Les Débuts de Chichine*. Her partners in this are unknown. The first performance took place on 19 December in Connecticut, at the New Haven Theatre, and was a disaster. The larger part of the audience comprised students from Yale University. That afternoon, an important football match had taken place between Yale and Princeton, and Yale had suffered a humiliating defeat. This, and the fact that the theatre manager had hiked ticket prices from 70 cents to $2 did not put them in a good mood to begin with, though they were assured that this had been necessary because Gaby had travelled all the way from Paris just to perform for them, which was not true.

When the curtain rose, hundreds of horny young men began chanting Gaby's name. Had the theatre manager had any sense he would have brought her on at once and allowed her to do *something* to open the show. Instead, the audience was subjected to ninety minutes of a first half comprising acts they had probably never heard of. She was cheered when she walked on after the interval, and after her first song, *Je chante la gloire de la Parisienne*. The students so loved *Tout en rose* that she was made to sing it again. Then she announced that though there would be several more songs and a couple of dance-routines later in the show, the local sheriff had deemed *Les Débuts de Chichine* immoral and ordered her to remove it from the programme. Upon hearing this, all hell broke loose. Gaby fled the stage, and locked herself in her dressing-room until the police arrived, whence she was bundled into the back of a van and driven back to her hotel, minutes before the riot squad arrived. Running amok, some of the students rushed the stage and an all-out brawl ensued between them and the stage hands. Within the auditorium, seats were smashed, chandeliers brought down, and the orchestra pit wrecked. The violence escalated when the fire brigade arrived and turned their hoses on the audience, drenching not just the offenders but those audience members unable to get away from the fracas. Weapons were drawn, forcing police officers to wade in with batons. Dozens of students were arrested, along with two members of the Yale football squad. And though the theatre was cleared, the trouble did not desist. Out in the street, students pelted the police with bottles and stones, and windows were smashed until the situation was finally brought under control. The Hyperion later announced that repairing the damage had cost them well over $1,000, and almost as much again in damages claims from members of the audience.

Early the next morning, Gaby boarded the train for New York, where there was an almighty showdown in Jake Shubert's 1416 Broadway office. Shubert tried to convince her that the cause of the brawl in New Haven had little to do with her—that if Yale had won their football match, it would have been the most magnificent evening of her career. This was partly true. Gaby agreed to give the Winter Garden a go but not without warning Shubert that if there were any more problems, she would return to France without delay. Fortunately for everyone involved, the greatest adventure of her life was waiting just around the corner.

*

Though she had attended the matinee performance at the Folies-Bergère, she had not yet met Harry, while he had only seen her in the press. Lee Shubert tried to whet his appetite by sending him copies of the publicity photographs supplied some time earlier by

Mariano Unzué—none had yet been taken of her American stage shows. If he was expecting Harry to be impressed he was in for a disappointment, while Harry steadfastly refused to work with Jolson. In the end, money came before personal pride, and he signed the contract.

Gaby and Harry met for the first time when she gave an interview in the dressing-room assigned to her at the Winter Garden, one week ahead of the rehearsals. Twenty or so "reporters" had crowded into the room—plants hired by Jake Shubert, armed with huge sprays of orchids and instructed to lavish her with praise for her talent and great beauty—while pleading with her not to leave New York. Harry brought only himself, and it was only after the fake press had left that she observed him sitting in a corner of the room. Audaciously, she asked why he had not brought her a gift—adding that her previous leading men had always given her an item of jewellery or some other costly trinket, their means of expressing their gratitude for having the privilege of working with her. Pointing to the heavy rope of pearls around her neck, Harry responded in an incomprehensible (to her) Bronx twang that only fools gave women baubles—an obvious reference to Manuel of Portugal—adding that his "gift" was worth more than all the pearls in the world. This game of cat-and-mouse lasted for a while, before Harry dropped the latch on the door. At first, Gaby was afraid. Mariano had warned her about Harry's unpredictable temper, and she had read about the incident with the electric fan in Sport Herman's office. Then Harry dropped his trousers, and revealed his surprise—he had tied a pink ribbon around his private parts. According to the story told by Gaby to Régine Flory, they then had sex on the carpet, setting in motion one of the most passionate love-affairs in the history of the music-hall. A few days later, Harry ended his relationship with his chorus-boy lover.

The next evening, Harry took Gaby to a jazz-club in Harlem, where he had picked up the latest dance crazes: the Foxtrot, the Turkey Trot, the Grizzly Bear, and the Bunny Hug. She was amazed by the suppleness of the black dancers, but shocked upon learning that, not only were black people banned from appearing on the New York stage, they were segregated from white audiences and, if they wanted to see a show, not allowed to pass through the front entrances of the theatres the same as everyone else. The first time she went on a train, she was horrified to see the "Whites Only" signs on some of the carriage doors. There was no such prejudice in France, and the fact that one section of America was discriminated against for the colour of their skin upset her profoundly.

Gaby and Harry joined the cast of *Vera Violetta* at the end of 1911, well into the 112-performance run. Neither was the revue the only item on the bill, though it did open the proceedings—Jake Shubert had learned his lesson after the New Haven fiasco, and this time when the orchestra struck up the overture and the mostly male audience began chanting Gaby's name, they were not disappointed. It must be noted that Harry, as the dashing playboy, Prince Fersen, received as many wolf-whistles of appreciation as she did. After the first interval came *Undine*, a one-act play set on an ice-skating rink and featuring swimmer-showgirl Annette Kellerman (1887-1975), a precursor of Esther Williams. The evening closed with an hour of vaudeville, of which *The Tribune* commented, "The less said the better…it does not deserve the valuable waste of space!"

Throughout their stay with the show, Gaby and Harry were mocked and harassed by Al Jolson—and initially by 18-year-old Mae West, who had made her stage debut in *A La Broadway*, the revue which had alternated with *Hello, Paris* at the Folies-Bergère but folded after just eight performances. Mae, who had clearly set her sights on Harry and attempted to upstage Gaby, was an easy problem to deal with—Gaby got her fired from the production because at the time she was not of great importance. Jolson was another matter entirely. He only had a supporting role as Claude, the blackface waiter in *Undine*, but stole the show from Annette Kellerman with his performances of *That Haunting Melody* and *Rum-Tum-Tiddle*, which he encored in the show's vaudeville section. Adolph Klauber of *The New York Times* observed, "Jolson, in the role of the coloured waiter, succeeded in rousing the audience into the first enthusiasm of the evening and kept them enthusiastic much of the time afterwards." The songs were so popular that he recorded them for Victor, in December 1911, his first visit to a studio.

The real show-stopper, however, was *The Gaby Glide*, a kind of *valse-chaloupée* performed to a noisy but exciting jazz accompaniment. The lyrics were by Harry and the piece was choreographed by him, though Ned Wayburn took the credits in the programme and on the playbills:

> Everybody's raving 'bout the real French two-step,
> Everybody wants to do this smart fancy new step,
> Well, I do declare it's classy...
> Prance along as though you were on the boulevard,
> And dance it there and keep on dancing hard...
> Oh! Oh! That Gaby, Gaby Glide!

On the evening they introduced *The Gaby Glide*, Gaby and Harry received a standing ovation longer than the piece itself, and were forced to repeat it. Jolson was having none of this. He had been on the bill and receiving rapturous applause long before they had been brought into the production, and was not about to let them steal his thunder. The next evening, while they were dancing, he walked on to the stage and stood behind them, limp-wristed and making faces. The audience cheered, thinking this part of the act. Harry confronted him in his dressing-room after the show, and threatened him with a good hiding, should he pull such a stunt again—more than this, unless Jolson behaved himself, he *would* to expose him as one of the men who had once paid to have sex with him. The singer complied, but only for now.

Gaby was earning a lot of money, but giving a lot away to various charitable institutions in New York. This may have gone unnoticed by scandalmongers of the press only interested in her love-life, and she herself may not have wanted the public to become aware of her benevolences, fearing that they would have been taken the wrong way. Though most of the critics loved *Vera Violetta*, Alan Dale still had an axe to grind, and writing this time for the *New York Journal* he not only condemned Gaby for her "gross lack of talent", but denounced her as "mercenary" in thinking of no one but herself. This infuriated her to the extent that she headed for the newspaper's office, and launched an egotistical counter-attack on Dale (in French, and subsequently translated by the editor) which if anything only made matters worse:

> I am called mercenary. Your Alan Dale has said that all I love is the dollar and all I think of is money. They say too that I cannot love, that I am too hard, too fond of money to love! I *am* mercenary! I take all I can and keep all I get! I give nothing back! I *can* love! It's in me to have that grand passion. When I have all the money I want, *then* I'll marry, and when I marry it will be for all time. Gaby Deslys will never figure in a divorce! The world will take all that a woman has and will give her nothing in return if she asks for nothing. But let her fix her price and stand by it, and the world will give her all she wants and ask to give

her more! When youth passes, when beauty fades, money is the only thing that helps a woman against the world. The rich woman has a natural barrier between herself and the world. Men pay more respect to my pearls than to my beauty or talent…Men say I'm beautiful, I'm magnetic. It may be true. If it is, then let me make the most of it! These things are of worth. If I give men the pleasures of them, men must pay for them. Beauty goes, magnetism fades. Money remains, *if* you're careful. Men expect me to give them my time for nothing. They expect me to sup with them, dine with them. My time is money. Any man who has a hundred, two-hundred dollars in his pocket thinks he can invite me to supper. Peef! If I want supper I can buy it for myself. I refuse. They sneer and say, "The little *miser*! The *mercenary*!"

The cheers and standing ovations, and the thrill of being revered by New York audiences could not compensate for Dale's latest attack, and adding insult to injury—and despite again being threatened with a pasting from Harry—Al Jolson began sabotaging Gaby's solo spots on the stage. One evening early in January 1912, while she was singing *Je chante la gloire de la Parisienne*, he appeared on stage behind her and began clowning around. Then, after running around her several times he leapt off the stage and dashed up and down the aisles, pulling faces at the audience. Again they thought it part of the act. There was an unpleasant incident with an unnamed man who sent a note to her dressing room—explaining he was a wealthy businessman, and inviting to "take a spin" with him in his airplane. Gaby refused, and he turned up again the following evening, inviting her to have supper with him after the show. To convince her that everything was "above board", he offered to take the *entire* 200-strong Winter

Garden company to her favourite restaurant—with the exception of Harry and Jolson. Thinking that her colleagues deserved a treat, Gaby agreed. After the meal, he asked her to get into his car and accompany him to his apartment. Gaby thanked him for his kindness, but declined. Several days later she received a visit from the restaurant manager, who presented her with a bill for $800. The man was an admirer who wanted to have sex with her and, after being snubbed he had asked the manager to charge everything to her. That same day she received bills for the flowers and brooch he had given her, and for the hire of the car in which he had hoped to take her home! He was arrested by the police, found guilty of fraud, and sentenced to three months in prison.

For Gaby, this was the last straw. She told Jake Shubert that she was leaving the production. Harry, who would have preferred to carry out his earlier threat and give Jolson a thrashing, added that he would be leaving with her. The next day, Gaby cabled Alfred Moul in London, and told him that she was ready to do a season at the Alhambra more or less at once—her only condition being that Harry share the bill. Less than one hour later, Moul cabled her back and offered her £325 a week. If this seemed paltry compared to what she was earning in New York, Gaby obviously thought that it would be worth taking a substantial cut in salary in order to achieve peace of mind. She argued against a clause in the contract which stated that her fee was for both matinee and evening performances, telling Moul that she would expect to receive her full fee whether she played matinees or not. His curt response to this was that she would not be welcome in his theatre again. Similarly, Jake Shubert informed Harry that if he left him in the lurch, he would never set foot in any of *his* theatres again. Harry was unperturbed. Gaby had already booked their passage to France. Mariano Unzué had negotiated with the Théâtre Femina, in Paris, for them to open in a revue on 2 February 1912.

On 17 January, Gaby and Harry boarded the *RMS Baltic*, taking with them the $65,000 Gaby had earned in America, forty trunks of luggage—two filled with gifts from admirers—a half-grown live crocodile, and a Negro maid supplied by Harry's bandleader brother, Murray. They were waved off by a huge crowd, which included not just fans but moralists and members of religious groups who, having been shocked by their "openly sinful" relationship, were pleased to be seeing the back of them. The editor of one of New York's best-selling "Bible-bashing" weeklies had taken a particular disliking of Harry:

> Why is Harry Pilcer permitted to make himself so obnoxiously conspicuous in a chorus number in which he TRIES to dance? WHO is Harry Pilcer, anyway? To judge by his performance, he is an amateur of the most pronounced type! Yet he is per-mitted to JOLLY the audience, the leader of the orchestra, and the principal players in the cast, as well as the chorus. In short, he is what in slang parlance would be called FRESH. He may be on the stage to win a bet, or he may be related to the management. Whatever the cause of his appearance may be, it is obviously unfair to both his audiences and his stage associates to inflict his FRESHNESS upon them for a period of ten minutes in the GABY GLIDE…with the EXCEPTION of this, it is only fair to say that the Winter Garden furnishes the best variety entertainment this side of the Atlantic.

The crossing was fraught with difficulties. The Negro maid is reported to have fallen overboard and drowned. The crocodile died during the voyage, though Gaby kept it and later had it stuffed. What annoyed the other passengers was the couple's habit of making love almost anywhere when the mood took them, which was apparently often. Harry hated confined spaces, and spent the first few days of the voyage on deck, enveloped in blankets and furs. One evening, the captain was asked to investigate a complaint and caught them having sex in one of the lifeboats, under Gaby's sable cloak. Next morning, the *RMS Baltic* stopped off at Queenstown (Cobh) in Ireland, and the couple were told that unless they promised to curb their "sinful behaviour" and stay in their cabin for the remainder of the journey, they would not be allowed back on the ship. Gaby called his bluff and argued that there was nothing sinful about their love-making—and showed the captain the certificate, stamped in Queenstown, stating that they had married during their brief hours ashore! She then threw a strop and declared that she would travel no further on the *RMS Baltic* after such an insult, and sailing was held up for two hours as a team of porters unloaded Gaby and Harry's luggage—generously rewarded for doing so—and transported it to the nearest hotel.

The next day, the couple booked passages on the night-boat to Liverpool. From here they travelled to Portsmouth, where they spent the night at a guest-house before sailing to Le Havre. Needless to say, when they arrived they were met with a barrage of press whose prime concern was "vetting" Gaby's latest acquisition—Harry Pilcer. She told reporters that by settling down with "an honest, normal man" she would be putting paid to the still-persistent rumours that her greatest ambition was to become queen of Portugal. Harry had no intention of settling down, and for the rest of his life would hang on to his freedom and his *garcons*, of which there would be many. The news of his marriage to Gaby, however, brought his American chorus-boy lover out of the closet and he was revealed to be Harold Singer, whose brother Mort had been Harry's agent at the time of *The Flirting Princess*.

Singer scoffed upon hearing that Harry had left New York to find fame in Europe, and was confident that he would return to the fold once Gaby had tired of him. Now, he realised that he had lost him for good. He told a New York reporter:

> Pilcer and I were very close. I knew him better than anyone, and I don't for one moment believe that he's married Gaby Deslys. And in any case, she's a Catholic and he's Jewish."

In London, the *Tatler* posed, while hinting at Gaby's reputation of being a lush, "What do you think of the rumour that Gaby Deslys has married an American dancer? No one believed it over here. We all know how practical young Gaby is."

The magazine and Harold Singer turned out to be right. On 29 January, within hours of reaching Paris, Gaby told one reporter that the wedding ceremony had never taken place—while Harry told another that it had. Suffice to say, there is no record of any marriage in the Queenstown archives. Anna Caire had her say when she read that Harry was thinking of converting to Catholicism so that he *could* marry her daughter. Religion had nothing to do with it, she declared—what perturbed her was that, not content with leading her daughter astray, Harry was now after her money!

Arguably, Harry's most famous creation.

Harry and Gaby in *Vera Violetta*.

Gaby and Harry in *Vera Violetta*.

6: *Honeymoon Express*

The Théâtre Femina, on the Rond Pont de Champs-Elysées, was a far cry from New York's Winter Garden. It was much smaller and more intimate, and because Gaby was on home territory she could do no wrong. In New York, Harry had taught her to dance properly, as opposed to executing coquettish movements which *she* had called dancing while pouting her lips at the wealthy toffs in the stalls. Incurably headstrong, Gaby had not taken such advice lightly and during rehearsals for the revue the backstage the rows were non-stop. Harry was the archetypal perfectionist, and not a patient man, and refused to put up with her tantrums—more than once, she felt the back of his hand though this only stimulated her sexual appetite, which like his was considerable. Paris audiences were introduced to the latest American dance crazes: the Turkey Trot, the Bunny Hug, the Grizzly Bear, and the Shiver featured in a section of the revue entitled *Deedledum*. Another tableau included a routine, *Viens danser*, which had audiences gasping as Harry tossed Gaby high into the air, then caught her inches from the floor. The piece was timed to the split-second and ended with them face-to-face, their lips separated by a hair's breath. Though Gaby and Harry never kissed on the stage, their body movements were considered lewd even by Parisians who had not been perturbed by witnessing the city's first bare breasts, recently displayed at the Moulin-Rouge. But if a handful of fuddy-duddies stormed out of the theatre when Harry peeled off his shirt and flexed his muscles, there were many men who caught their breath in amazement. In next to no time he had attracted the largest gay following Paris had ever known.

The Femina revue closed at the end of February, and Gaby and Harry travelled to London. Anna Caire and Mariano Unzué were still living at Number Three, which must have made life uncomfortable as neither could stand Harry. Gaby's mother was hoping that his success in Paris would prove a flash in the pan and that he would soon be returning to New York—Mariano confident that when this happened, Gaby would come running back to him. It was he, acting as her manager, who negotiated the Deslys-Pilcer contract with Alfred Butt of the Palace Theatre. Their combined salary for *Mademoiselle Chichi* was not made public, but is said to have been the largest ever offered to a variety act. During their three days in London the couple were trailed by reporters each vying for an exclusive on their "marriage". The 7 February issue of the *Sketch Supplement* had carried four "shocking" photographs wired from the Apeda Studio in New York and these now appeared in other publications. One depicted Harry, wearing a vest and pressing an "alarmed" Gaby over the back of a marble bench, while she attempted to claw at his perfectly pomaded hair.

As their partnership continued, the photographs of Gaby and Harry became more controversial. The Atelier Reutlinger, on the boulevard Montmartre, was founded by Charles Reutlinger in 1850, and for many years was frequented by Paris's *honorable société*. His nephew Léopold took over the studio in 1890, and among the changes he made was the introduction of "naughty" postcards of famous celebrities—considered puerile at the time and mostly sold under the counter, but tame by today's standards. Léopold had famously photographed the dancer Mata-Hari in a harem costume, with her breasts enclosed in jewelled metal cups. His study of La Belle Otéro had revealed her exposing a fleshy thigh and ruby-studded suspender with one hand, while the other had been in the act of moving her gusset to one side to expose her vagina. Reutlinger's most celebrated photograph of Gaby was not taken at his studio, however, but in her dressing-room while her maid was adjusting her garter.

Off-stage, Harry was much more narcissistic than on, and had no reservations when stripping off for the camera. Léopold Reutlinger, however, refused to photograph any man in any state of undress. Things progressed much further in the middle of March when Gaby and Harry played a short season at the Apollo, in Vienna—more or less a series of dress-rehearsals for the London revue. One afternoon they paid a visit to the Studio Atelier-Weit, where Harry was photographed in a white tattered shirt, bending Gaby backwards over his knee. Subsequently mass-produced, it sold thousands of copies. Such was the furore that the studio issued a statement declaring the other photographs from the session had been deemed *so* indecent that the manager had ordered them to be destroyed. This was not true. In one, Harry crouches on the floor in a submissive pose, his shirt still ripped to shreds, while Gaby stands over him menacingly, in a skirt he has slashed to the waist. In another he wears a jewelled posing-pouch, and is bent backwards over a lump of rock, his groin thrust upwards inches from her lips. Others depicted him totally naked.

A set of these photographs landed on the desk of renowned theatre critic Paul Renaison (1895-1953), who wrote for *Gil Blas* under the pseudonym Jean Ernest-Charles. In an extended feature in the 21 June issue, he accused Gaby of being responsible for a decline in music-hall morals, and of achieving fame and fortune not by way of talent, but by taking advantage of an "innocent under-aged king". He went on:

> She is a pretty girl, and brilliant—in that she does not know how to sing or dance, and for having a repertoire of crude English tunes with Negro lyrics. To solidify her position [in America] she was obliged to pay special attention to the wild voters of Colonel Cody [President Theodore] Roosevelt. Her beauty is cosmopolitan and her

accent undefinable, that of a stevedore! She does not dance, she *exposes* herself. She wrecks everything: music, harmony, words. *Nothing* works where she is concerned. She is a joke!

Outraged—especially by Renaison's hint that she was little more than a prostitute—and without telling Harry she paid the journalist a visit and informed him that unless he published a retraction in the periodical's next issue, she would hire someone to horsewhip him *and* sue him for 50,000 francs for character assassination! Renaison refused to be blackmailed, and wrote a *second* article—thanking Gaby for now presenting him with the opportunity to clear the air in a court of law. He was defended in the press by Henri Bidou of the celebrated weekly cultural publication, *Journal des Débats*, who praised him for his honest opinion, and added an opinion of his own—by achieving fame the way she had, Gaby Deslys should be deemed a crime against the State!

Gaby lost the case and the court ordered her to pay Renaison undisclosed damages. She refused to let the matter rest, and tried to badger Harry into taking out a lawsuit against Renaison to fight for her honour. He refused, and her reaction was to threaten to fire him from her "company"—to be reminded that he was not hers for hiring and firing, and that after the New Haven fiasco *she* had only become a big name in America because of her partnership with him. Mariano Unzué then dropped another bombshell. He had been negotiating with Jake and Lee Shubert for another season in New York, to which had been added a clause that if she performed in the United States again, it would have to be with Harry, or not at all, because he was by far the bigger star. Needless to say, she quickly backed down.

The controversy did not affect Gaby's career, while Harry did not care one way or the other if it did—Jake Shubert was cabling him every other day, begging him to return to New York, with or without his "wife" and forgetting that he had vowed never to have him in one of his theatres again. In July, the couple put on a show at the Femina—an overnight dance competition organised by Harry, which began at midnight and lasted until six in the morning. They opened the proceedings with the Argentine Tango, the first time this was performed in Europe. After the prizes had been handed out to the winners, the gala ended with the *apache*, which saw Gaby emulating the Atelier-Weit photographs and ripping the shirt off Harry's back while the audience went wild.

There was more drama when Gaby and Harry travelled to Deauville for a weekend break. Mariano Unzué had moved out of Number Three, tired of the constant tension between the lovers and Anna Caire, though he was still Gaby's agent. One evening, after supper, Gaby and Harry were strolling along the resort's celebrated *planches* when they bumped into Mariano and Arlette Dorgère, in whose revue Gaby had appeared at the Théâtre Femina back in 1904. Gaby tried not to show her displeasure when Mariano announced that he was living with her in her chateau at Vigneux-sur-Seine, ten miles south of Paris. What she did not know was that they had been lovers for some time, even while Mariano had been with her.

From Deauville, Gaby and Harry headed for Calais, then on to London. The first Royal Variety Performance had taken place at the Palace Theatre on 1 July 1912, in the presence of George V and Queen Mary. Headlining had been Harry Lauder and the dancer Anna Pavlova. Alfred Butt had wanted Gaby and Harry to perform a brief sketch, but with Marie Lloyd their names were at the top of Buckingham Palace's "vulgarity" list—the male impersonator Vesta Tilly made the bill but the Queen, disgusted at seeing a woman wearing trousers, covered her face with her programme while she was on stage.

With an only slightly amended title, *Mademoiselle Chic* opened on 26 August. Gaby and Harry's 25-minute sketch, *A Day in Trouville*, shared the bill with the usual line-up of singers, clowns and comedians, and with Annette Kellerman reviving *Undine* which had proved so popular in New York. The pre-publicity photographs were published in *The Sketch*, but in the wake of the Atelier-Weit controversy suitably tamed down. Gaby was depicted in elaborate, full-length gowns, and Harry not at all. The storyline was routine. Yvonne, a pretty *demimondaine*, has to choose between having a loving relationship with wet-behind-the-ears working-class boy Billy (Harry)—or accepting money from the wayward Hickson (Pierre Létol). While making her choice, she sings several ditties and engaged in any number of elaborate dance routines with the former. Part of the bedroom scene from *Les Débuts de Chichine* was incorporated into the piece, with Gaby getting in and out of bed in a succession of flimsy nighties, and at one stage stripping out of her evening gown and dancing around the bed in her underwear—causing some fussier members of the audience to walk out. This routine was dropped after the first week, and replaced by *The Gaby Glide*, and a ballet sketch for which Gaby wore a tutu covered in dozens of tiny wings, and a headdress covered in cherries. A photograph from this appeared on the cover of *The Sketch*.

Elsewhere in the city, the Alhambra's Alfred Moul—who had vowed never to have Gaby in his theatre again—was pulling in the crowds with *The Guide To Paris*, in which singer May Flower impersonated Gaby at the time of the Manuel scandal. Both she and Harry were parodied in *Everybody's Doing It*, at the Empire. In this, Ida Crispi played Gaby—teaching Robert Hale, impersonating Harry impersonating Sir Francis Drake—how to do *The Gaby Glide*. Gaby does not appear to have minded these skits, perhaps because she was not the only French star being sent up—

"Mistinguett" and "Polaire" were also on the Alhambra bill. She did object to Alfred Butt's taking a leaf out of Moul's book by adding Manuel's portrait to the on-stage props of *Mademoiselle Chic*, and even though this was taken down after being used for just one performance, she stopped giving interviews so as to avoid having to answer any awkward questions.

The revue closed at the end of October, and on 1 November 1912 Gaby and Harry left for Liverpool. With them were two marmosets—Chichine and Alphonse—presented to Gaby by fans. Harry, who appears to have still been sleeping around despite the "are they or aren't they married?" speculation, had been given a "special pet" by a male admirer—a large teddy bear which he carried everywhere, and with which he posed for photographs next morning on the gangplank of the *RMS Caronia*, famed for sending the first ice warning to the ill-fated *Titanic*, earlier in the year. A day into the crossing, a sailor named Jerry Shea fell from the crow's nest and was badly hurt. Gaby personally tended his injuries, and made a collection on board for his family so that they would not suffer hardship while he was off work—while Harry enjoyed a fling with one of Shea's mariner friends.

The news of Gaby's good deed and Harry's antics was relayed to New York. It was his appearance, however, and not Gaby's furs, monkeys and jewels which surprised the welcoming committee in New York—clutching his teddy bear, he was wearing a bright yellow suit and matching trilby. When one of the reporters sniggered at him over his appearance, he marched up to him and threatened to thump him.

Gaby had a fit of pique with a reporter who asked about her wedding, yelling at him, "There was no wedding. It's all lies!" Another held up a newspaper which had their picture on the front page, under the headline, "Gaby & Harry Wed", and read aloud from the accompanying feature of how Gaby's mother had issued a statement in Paris declaring that Gaby and Harry *had* married, because Gaby had sent her a cable confirming this.

There were problems in the customs-hall—the twenty-six trunks within which Gaby had hidden her jewels, including Manuel's pearls, were confiscated because officials refused to believe that the contents had been valued in excess of $330,000. Tempers became frayed as the couple were forced to wait until an independent assessor had been brought in to verify this. Once this had been sorted out, they were driven to the railway station where *The Gaby Express*, a specially adapted carriage, awaited them.

Harry lost his cool when he and Gaby checked into their hotel, and Jake Shubert called them to lay down the law. Both had rebelled against the terms of the pre-*Vera Violetta* contract by leaving him in the lurch and going to France. Now, to teach them a lesson, and to make up for upsetting Al Jolson—when it had been the other way around—they were to augment his touring revue, *A Social Whirl*, a truncated version of the show (*The Whirl of Society*) which had played at the Winter Garden earlier in the year. Gaby and Harry were told that they would be joining the company when it reached Pittsburgh the following week. Shubert concluded that he would meet them the next day to discuss their salaries, and hung up.

The next morning when Shubert arrived at the hotel, Gaby and Harry had moved out. He located them a few hours later at the Pilcers' house in Manhattan's West 111th Street. Elsie and Samuel, who obviously cared more for Gaby than the Caires did about their son, had welcomed her with open arms and were far from pleased with Shubert's bullying tactics. They informed him that Gaby and Harry were ill in bed—in separate rooms. Shubert did not believe this, and the Pilcers were asked to give the couple a message. Gaby had been forgiven, but Harry still owed the showman twenty performances that he had missed by following her to France, and unless he fulfilled his obligations, now that he had tricked him back on to American soil, he would be arrested and sued. The showman dropped another bombshell. There had been a change of plan and they would be expected to join the Jolson revue, at Trenton, New Jersey—that very evening! On the plus side, Shubert added, in their 30-minute segment they would not be expected to perform new routines, only those they had done in London, though the evening would close with *The Gaby Glide*.

Gaby and Harry arrived at the theatre with less than an hour to spare before curtain-up. Shubert was waiting in the wings but this time Gaby was holding the aces. In a hasty reprinting, the names Deslys and Pilcer now appeared on the playbills and posters above Al Jolson's, and all the tickets for the evening performance had sold in record time, necessitating folding seats being placed in the aisles. Gaby told Shubert that she would not step on to the stage until he had agreed to increase their salaries—hers from $4,000 a week to $5,000, and Harry's to $3,000. On the face of it this was unfair, as Harry was also doing all the choreography, but it was twice the fee that Shubert was paying Jolson which was for Harry a victory over this homophobic man. Shubert agreed.

The ensuing tour was a great success, playing to packed houses in Buffalo, Baltimore, Philadelphia and Washington, and even progressing as far as Montreal in Canada. It grossed $150,000 in five weeks, a record at the time, and closed in January 1913, by which time Shubert had set the wheels in motion for a brand new revue at the Winter Garden, imposing a three-week rehearsal period which Harry said was not long enough for him to devise new dance routines. Shubert placated him by raising his salary once more, to $4,000, but there were conditions. Gaby's name would be in lights, and Harry and Al Jolson would share *equal* billing. Harry agreed. He needed as much money he could make in as short a time as possible, he told Shubert, because after the revue he would be leaving America for good. This was the first that Gaby had heard of this, and she was delighted because she assumed that he would be returning to France with her. In fact, he had received an offer from the Palace Theatre, in London, to headline his own revue with a partner of his choice—and he had already decided that this would not be Gaby.

The Honeymoon Express opened on 6 February 1913, and caused mass hysteria among its first audiences, who had never seen anything quite like this one. Set in France, its most innovative scene featured a race between an automobile and the express train of the title. The *New York Globe*'s Louis Sherwin's review took up an entire page, and included stunning photographs of the leads: Gaby and Harry, Al Jolson, Fanny Brice, Harry Fox, and a little-known newcomer named Yansci Dolly who was married to Fox, and who had much in common with Harry. Like him, she and her twin sister Roszicka were the offspring of a Budapest tailor who had settled on New York's Lower East Side. As the infamous Dolly Sisters—Jenny and Rosie—they would leave a string of broken hearts and wrecked marriages wherever they went. In 1941, Jenny would hang herself from the shower-rail in her apartment. Rosie, like Gaby, would spend the last years of her life putting on charity shows to benefit the poor. Sherwin observed:

> When one remembers how few things she could do when she first arrived here last year, and how many she can do now, one knows that Miss Deslys is a person to be reckoned with, particularly in the last act with Harry Pilcer in *When Gaby Did The Gaby Glide*. Pilcer also dances with one Yansci Dolly *The Original Bacchanale*, and the music is by Borodin. This takes place on the grand staircase at the Paris Opera, although it defies description. It's not a Turkey Trot nor Isadora Duncaning nor staircase

> waltzing, nor even Russian dancing. It is perhaps the Kosloffering of Pilcer and Dolly, and when you see that subtle lady slide down the banisters head first and do a few other things besides, you may have the self-same shiver down your spine that went down this writer's. The scene which gives the play its name occurs at the end of the first act, when there is a race between an automobile and a train. From the first faint glimmer of distant lights way up on the mountainside, through the devious turns of the road, down the valleys and onto the level stretch, into tunnels and out of them, and finally right down to the footlights with a rush and a roar, and almost into the audience!

According to Al Jolson's biographer, Herbert G. Goldman, this section of the revue was filmed, though the quarter-reel short, like Gaby and Harry's other filmed work, does not appear to have survived:

> The final scene of Act 1 of *The Honeymoon Express* consisted of a frantic race between an automobile driven by Gus (Jolson), with Baudrey (Pilcer), Yvonne (Deslys) and Mme de Bressie (Ada Lewis) as passengers, and a train travelling to Rouen on which Henri Dubonet (Ernest Glendenning) is supposedly a passenger. The film, which depicted the chase, ended with the car and train about to pull into Rouen at the same time. On the stage, the screen was raised, the lights came on, and the orchestra struck its final notes as both the car and train were shown beside each other at Rouen station.

The success of the revue and the nightly standing ovation received by *The Gaby Glide*, failed to compensate for Harry's anger over Jake Shubert's hiring of Ernest Glendenning to play Gaby's lover, and throughout the run he would have nothing to do with him. Within a week, the box-office takings had exceeded $30,000, but if everyone looked like they were having great fun, such was the ill-feeling amongst the company that few of the cast were on speaking terms extant of when they were on stage.

Gaby performed three songs in the show. *When The Honey Moon Stops Shining, You'll Call The Next Love The First* and *Bring Back Your Love* have not survived the passage of time. *My Yellow Jacket Girl* is remembered by Jolson devotees, along with the oddity, *Who Paid The Rent For Mrs. Rip Van Winkle?* Joe McCarthy and Jimmy Monaco's *You Made Me Love You* stayed in his repertoire for the rest of his life, though Judy Garland's version, sung to a photograph of Clark Gable, remains definitive.

The song also proved prophetic for Harry. One evening, when Jolson was unable to go on stage and the role of Gus was played by his understudy, it was Harry who performed it. Though his voice was not as far-reaching as Jolson's, his vocal abilities were well above average. He directed the lyrics to a young man sitting on the front row, and after the show the two met in Harry's dressing-room. Gaby was told that he was a "friend of the family", and she did not object when Harry announced he would be spending the night at the Pilcers' Manhattan home. She was tired of all the arguments, and also had an admirer—an unnamed Wall Street stockbroker. After Harry left with his new friend, she went out to supper with hers, and for several weeks vaudeville's "hottest" couple went their separate ways. Gaby's association with her wealthy admirer ended in tragedy, however, when he proposed marriage one evening after supper and she turned him down—he rushed out of the restaurant and out into the street, took a gun from his pocket and shot himself dead.

This incident, and Al Jolson's renewed bullying in the wake of it, prompted Gaby to cable her mother and announce that she would be returning to France sooner than anticipated—alone, as Harry had been assigned to a revue which would open in Chicago when *The Honeymoon Express* closed. Anna Caire told her to stay put—that there was no way she was going to allow her to cross the Atlantic on her own. She arrived in New York on 17 March, St Patrick's Day, and their meeting was filmed by the Universal Manufacturing Company, and broadcast on cinema screens across America as part of their *Animated Weekly* newsreel series.

Harry, meanwhile, cancelled the Chicago revue and rushed to Gaby's side, as would always happen in times of strife. Their final performance at the Winter Garden took place on 18 April and was followed by a sumptuous party to which everyone in the cast was invited—except Al Jolson. A few days later, the couple and Anna Caire left New York. *The Honeymoon Express* soldiered on until 14 June, with Jolson topping the bill and Grace La Rue replacing Gaby in the role of Yvonne.

A tamer, less costly version of the revue, without most of the special effects, opened at the Paris Alhambra in June 1913, and this time Harry was able to occupy centre-stage without being hampered by Al Jolson, and offer his own interpretation of *You Made Me Love You*. For another twenty years, though they would never meet again, Harry and Jolson would perform each other's songs. The revue closed at the end of July, by which time Gaby and Harry had negotiated with Alfred Butt to open at London's Palace Theatre in Dion Clayton Calthrop's *Two Cafés And A Street*—the prefix, *A La Carte*", would later be added to the title.

Those provocative poses!

And more of the same!

7: *The Little Parisienne*

Gaby decided that *A La Carte* would be her best British revue ever, and from her base at Number Three set about organising her costumes. Anna Caire was still living here, but moved out when Harry moved in. It is possible that she resented him because, while in New York, she had been made aware of his homosexuality. Even so, she did not go too far away. As Kerville, Matichon was now performing on the stage, a song-and-dance patter not unlike that of her elder sister, though not with much success. Matichon had an apartment in Pigalle, to which Anna relocated. Gaby drafted her in to help out with the costumes all the same, and the atmosphere cannot have been too convivial—particularly as Harry had the habit of parading around the kitchen naked every morning, after his shower, while preparing Gaby's breakfast, mindless of who else might have been in the room.

The Gaby-Harry liaison may have been intensely sexual, initially, with both parties on the rebound from their respective affairs. In Paris, this changed because the French music-hall was more liberated than its American counterpart. There was much less discretion as Harry found men of all ages literally throwing themselves at him. From this point, the physical side of their relationship would diminish, and eventually cease altogether, though they would remain the closest of friends until the very end.

The revue opened on 4 August, with a fanfare of publicity. A massive hoarding above the Palace Theatre entrance depicted Gaby, and the announcement, "SHE'S BACK!" in ten feet high letters. It was not an easy run. Harry almost walked out of the production when Alfred Butt informed him at the eleventh hour that he would not be singing *You Made Me Love You.* This honour went to Grace La Rue, who had replaced Gaby in *The Honeymoon*

Express and who Butt brought over from New York. Harry's response was to stroll on to the stage each evening after she had finished and announce, "Thank you, *Stella Parsons!*"—La Rue's real name, which she hated. Gaby had a fit of pique upon learning that Manuel of Portugal was about to marry Augusta-Victoria of Hohensollern-Sigmaringen, his cousin and a descendent of the kings of Prussia. The wedding took place on 5 September, and photographs show the couple looking deliriously happy. They remained so until Manuel's death in 1932, aged 43. Aware that Harry preferred other men, Gaby had always hoped that she and Manuel would be reunited.

Gaby's costumes for *A La Carte*, though outrageous at the time, would today be regarded as silly. Most were designed by Etienne Drian and Landolff—the latter had worked for Polaire when Gaby had first seen her in Marseille. The most ridiculous outfit comprised a pair of multicoloured Oriental trousers, over which Gaby wore a tasselled lamp-shade skirt. Another exposed much of her bosom, was cut short at the front, and ended in a fishtail at the back. There were also several hobble-skirts, so tight that she could hardly walk in them, let alone dance. The feathered headdresses were by the Maison Lewis, who had a shop on Regent Street. The Palace audiences loved every minute of this extreme exhibitionism, and even the critics were not over-condemning when the show opened. Some members of the clergy were not impressed. The Bishop of Kensington, John Maud, was not comfortable with Gaby staying at a hotel in his diocese, and since the Manuel scandal had been looking for a way of getting back at her. One evening he sent one of his representatives to the Palace, who reported back how offended he had been watching the "gross indecency" of the latest dance craze. Harry had adapted the Argentinian Tango, being performed for the first time on a British stage. The Bishop sent a letter of complaint to William Mansfield, the Lord Chamberlain, without seeing the show for himself, and this resulted in Alfred Butt being threatened with loss of license. There were further concerns when the Lord Chamberlain received a second complaint concerning the staircase sequence. In this, Gaby and Harry danced up and down the structure with astonishing athleticism, executing a series of near-cartwheels and contortions, finally ending up before the footlights with Gaby's legs wrapped around Harry's waist, according to the complaint, "as though engaged in an act of the most perverted fornication".

Alfred Butt was adamant in his response to the Lord Chamberlain that no activity had taken place on *any* of his stages which could be denounced as indecent, and that anything untoward had been but a figment of the Bishop of Kensington's perverted imagination. This raised the Bishop's hackles, and he insisted that if the Lord Chamberlain did not have the good sense to close the theatre, then he should at least force Alfred Butt to remove Gaby and Harry from the revue, which was by this time into the fifth of its ten-week run. Gaby's response was to send a note to the Bishop, asking him to come and see the show for himself instead of sending an "underling" to do his dirty work. Butt further argued that such dances were taking place in theatres across London, and that the Bishop had singled his star out for no other reason than she was Gaby Deslys. Astonishingly, the couple found an unlikely ally in George Bernard Shaw, who defended them in a letter to *The Times*, part of which read:

> The Bishop of Kensington is assuming what he approves of is right and what he disapproves of as wrong. He will have to admit that his epithet of "objectionable" merely means "disliked by the Bishop of Kensington". Miss Gaby Deslys is therefore just as entitled to the benefit of the doubt as the Bishop! Her means of entertainment has

proved highly attractive to large numbers of people whose taste is entitled to the same consideration as his own!

With such defence, Gaby and Harry were allowed to finish their run unimpeded, though Bernard Shaw declined to meet her. Speaking up for her was one thing, but being seen publicly with her was another, suggesting that his correspondence to *The Times* was but an attempt for him to edge his way into the untried field of the musical revue. If this was so, it failed. *The Music Cure*, a sketch from which Shaw drew his inspiration from Gaby, would open at the Palace in April 1914, and be trashed by the critics.

One introduction which took place at the Palace Theatre in October 1913 opened the door to a very bizarre liaison which remains as baffling today as back then. J. M. (James Matthew) Barrie was born in Kirriemur, Scotland, in 1860, and twenty-five years later moved to London to work as a journalist. In 1888, after the publication of his first book, *Auld Licht Idylls*, he gained acclaim as a novelist and playwright. His most famous work, *Peter Pan*, appeared in a book of short stories in 1902, and two years later transferred to the stage. His inspiration for this came from his visits to Kensington Gardens, where he spent hours delighting children and their parents with stories about the fairy he claimed he had seen land on the Serpentine. What these parents did not know was that, privately, Barrie was a morose and unhappy individual, and not as respectable as they were led to believe. His marriage had not been consummated, and he was amorously involved with the playwright Guy de Maurier, five years his junior. The son of the actor-manager Gerald du Maurier and the brother of Sylvia Llewelyn Davies, Guy had served in the Second Boer War, and been awarded the Distinguished Service Order. After the early deaths of Sylvia and her barrister husband, Arthur, Guy had been appointed co-guardian, with Barrie, of their five sons aged between seven and seventeen. It was George, found "roaming around the park like a lost little dog" when just five years old and later fostered by him, who became the great love of Barrie's life. For this reason, as much as he was admired for his literary genius, there were many—Harry Pilcer was but one—who regarded him as a paedophile.

When someone informed Harry that Barrie had sodomised a child, he saw no reason not to believe the allegation, did his utmost to discourage Gaby from seeing him, and the pair were forced to meet at Barrie's flat in Adelphi Terrace. When the writer offered to buy Gaby a chinchilla coat, she asked him to write her a short sketch instead, on the lines of *Peter Pan*. This was incorporated into *A La Carte*, though Barrie insisted that his name should not appear in the programme and on playbills. Harry went along with this to keep the peace. The London revue was drawing to a close, and he and Gaby had been invited back to New York by Jake Shubert—who swore that any animosity between them was now very firmly assigned to the past.

Early In November, the couple boarded the *Mauritania*. Gaby told reporters that she was leaving a greater part of her heart and soul behind her in England, and meant it. Then Harry smothered a smile as she added, "Tell the Bishop of Kensington that I love him, even if he *does* show a little too much leg!"

In New York, there were again issues with customs. This time the problem concerned Gaby's collection of rare, expensive plumes, valued at a staggering $25,000. In the wake of complaints from conservation societies who claimed that some species of wild birds were being wiped out to satisfy the whims of fashion houses, recent legislation prohibited such feathers from being brought into the country. After some deliberation, Gaby was allowed through customs, but only after signing a declaration that she would not leave any of the offending items behind when she left for France.

There were further problems with her pets. The marmosets had been replaced by two Mexican Chihuahuas which had snapped at everyone during the voyage—including Harry who had threatened to throw them overboard. There was also a pet hen which Gaby told reporters she had brought with her to ensure that she always had a fresh egg for breakfast! She and Harry were caught trying to smuggle them into the no-animals-allowed Astor Hotel, and after bawling out the manager they were taken to Claridge's, where they entered into negotiations with Jake Shubert, who was given an ultimatum by Harry—should he be thinking about putting them into the same revue as Al Jolson, he and Gaby would be returning to France on the next ship. Shubert had no such plans, though some of the artistes lined up to work with him and Gaby during their forthcoming winter tour would turn out to be as bad as Jolson, if not worse.

Harold Atteridge's *The Little Parisienne* opened at the Alvin Theatre, Pittsburgh on 24 November 1913, and the subsequent tour took in St Louis, Salt Lake City, San Francisco, Kansas City, Los Angeles, and Winnipeg's Walker Theatre. Like most of its predecessors, its story was trite and of secondary interest to audiences who, having read of the latest "gross indecency" case in London, were mostly interested in seeing how far Gaby and Harry would go with their dancing and on-stage antics. Only her picture appeared on the playbills which pronounced her "A Flashing Meteor In a Pleiades of Pearls". The critic with the *Manitoba Free Press* observed:

> It would take columns to describe the marvellous confections to which [Gaby], like a veritable bird of paradise, flitted about the stage of the Walker Theatre last night and with wonderfully piquant personality, entranced the masculine mind, while she threw the feminine part of

the audience into green spasms. A vivid green cloak over a pink *decolletté* gown, surmounted with two feet of pink ostrich plumes; a great shiny dazzle of gold; a leopard skin cloak, topped by pyramids of black feathers; a combi-nation of scarlet and black, daintily ornamented with medallions of blue and green, with cap to match; beautiful sables and chinchilla, and hats a yard in diameter, a flimsy white creation, with just a simple band of lilac; tiaras of gold, ropes of pearls, clusters of diamonds—such are some of the impressions made on the mere man...She succeeds absolutely in her two aims—to charm her audience and to startle them. With Harry Pilcer she executes a number of weird, sensuous dances of a character to make the persecuted tango appear, in comparison, a sanctimonious model of propriety. Mr. Pilcer is a pretty youth, something of the spoiled darling, with a shock of chestnut hair, and the smile of one who finds life worthwhile. Gaby Deslys speaks and sings in broken English, she says "zat" for that, "nussing" for nothing, "somesing" for something. Flirtation with her is a perfected art, and osculation a constant habit. The kissing is as much a feature of *The Little Parisienne* as is the dancing. Everyone kisses. Never was so much kissing done on the Walker stage in one evening.

Also on the bill was Evelyn Nesbit (1884-1967), no less controversial than Gaby. At fourteen she had fallen for 47-year-old architect-socialite Stanford White—after he had sexually abused her while she had been unconscious. She had gone on to have a passionate affair with actor John Barrymore, aborted his baby, and had finally married Harry Kendall Thaw (1871-1947), heir to a $40 million coal and railroad fortune—a drunkard, drug-addicted psychotic individual who had insisted that she wore black for their wedding ceremony, and who it later emerged got his kicks out of lashing her with a whip as a prelude to sex. While married, Nesbit had kept seeing White, and their stormy association had ended dramatically in June 1906 when Thaw had shot him dead in the rooftop theatre of Madison Square Garden. Declared insane at his trial, instead of going to the electric chair he had been committed to an asylum. Their Hollywoodized story made it several times to the big screen—most famously in *Ragtime* (1981), 81-year-old wheelchair-bound James Cagney's final outing in which Nesbit was played by Elizabeth McGovern, who gets to dance with Harry Pilcer (John Carrafa) at the beginning and end of the film.

Nesbit and Harry danced together in one segment of the revue, which after the Pittsburgh premiere he decided was once too often when she was unable to stop herself from "grabbing a handful". Even so, she pursued him throughout the tour, to such an extent that he is alleged to have slept with her just to stop her from pestering him.

Gaby was growing increasingly concerned about the constant changing of venues—the fact that no sooner had she settled in at one hotel than she was packing her trunks and heading back to the railway station—and the lengthy train journeys. When the short season in a bitterly cold Winnipeg ended on 14 January 1914, she called Jake Shubert, and told him that she had had enough and asked to "buy out" the remaining thirteen weeks of her contract. Of late her health had improved slightly, but she was still terrified of falling ill, worse still of dying in a foreign country. Shubert talked her around by offering her and Harry a three-week season in Chicago. For his sake, she agreed. This was his favourite American city, the one that had kick-started his career.

In Chicago, Gaby took advantage of Harry's high spirits by asking him to marry her. The response was not surprising. He told her that, despite finding her the most attractive woman in the world, he always would prefer having sex with men. He then gave her his solemn word that, no matter what happened, he would never desert her so long as she turned a blind eye to his amorous activities. What is equally remarkable is that though the couple continued sleeping together, off and on over the next few years—and though Harry had a succession of lovers of both sexes—Gaby never cheated on him while they were sexually active. Her days as "the world's most expensive whore" were well and truly over.

Some of vaudeville's biggest stars were appearing in Chicago when Gaby and Harry arrived in March. Gaby went to see Harry Lauder (1870-1950), but though she admired his act she could not work out his thick Scots accent and decided he would not prove much of a threat. Eva Tanguay (1878-1947) was a fiery-tempered, redhead who had made her name with raucous, risqué songs such as *It's All Been Done Before, But Not The Way I Do It*. Her biggest hit was *I Don't Care*, later immortalised by Judy Garland. If she had a bad day and the audience heckled her, which they inevitably did, *she* pelted *them* with rotten fruit. Even so, she was a massive crowd-puller and in her day the highest-paid female entertainer on the circuit, earning over $3,000 a week. Until Gaby came along, that is. The renowned show business historian Douglas Gilbert observed in 1940, when she was coming to the end of her career:

> It was impossible to overestimate Tanguay's personality or her influence in vaudeville. In the years she was the tops, this astonishing woman jolted the maudlin period of the 1900s away from its eye-dabbing with the vigour of unashamed sex, and by screaming, "*I want someone to go wild with me!*" This electrified hoyden got more sex into her shouted numbers than could be found in a crib street in a mining town.

Tanguay had a way with publicity. What she could not attract by her riotous lifestyle she paid for by taking out full-page advertisements in the press. She dealt with rival artistes who had the misfortune to be appearing in the same town—as happened with Gaby and Harry—by sending hecklers into the theatres where they were playing, usually armed with something to throw at the stage. Tanguay hated Gaby for no other reason than she was earning more than she was, and when Harry found out who was behind the calls of "sissy" from the galleries, he decided to "have it out" with her. Barging into her dressing-room he let rip, only to make a hasty exit when the powerfully-built Tanguay threatened to "rearrange" his face unless *he* stopped *bullying* her!

Lastly, there was Gertrude Hoffman (1886-1966), who later founded The Hoffman Girls. Not only did Hoffman dance and sing, she was an accomplished mimic whose send-ups of Eva Tanguay and Gaby had audiences in stitches. It was however her (unnamed) dance partner who raised Gaby's hackles with his high-camp impersonation of "Harry Pilsner". Gaby immediately applied for a court injunction. She won her case, and after removing the offending skit Hoffman made a public apology to Harry, who in all probability could not have cared less.

The Chicago revue closed, and Gaby and Harry returned to New York, where another headache awaited them. Jake Shubert had acquired the rights to an old musical-comedy, *The Girl from Kays*, a big hit in London in 1902 with Ethel Irving in the central role of Winnie Harborough, the salesgirl from Kays' hat shop. The story told of a couple who are about to set off on their honeymoon when the wife's new hat is delivered by Winnie. She is an old friend of the husband, and congratulates him with a kiss, setting in motion a number of nonsensical incidents. Shubert naturally wanted Gaby to play the flighty Winnie, and when she objected to the title, claiming it did not sound sufficiently romantic, and it was changed to *The Belle of Bond Street*. Shubert presented her with the script and when she observed that there was no part in it for Harry, she tore it up and announced that she would be leaving for Paris the next day. Knowing that he stood to lose a small fortune, and eager to exploit her as much as possible before her contract expired, Shubert effected a hasty rewriting of the script—Harry was cast as playboy Jack Richley, and asked to choreograph the dance routines. The second male lead was British-born actor Sam Bernard (1863-1927), who had played American Max Hoggenheimer, the American millionaire whom Winnie ended up with, in the 1903 Broadway production and its sequel, *The Rich Max Hoggenheimer*.

One gets the impression that Jake Shubert, weary of having his every decision opposed by this tetchy woman—not caring if she returned to America or not—*deliberately* set out to teach Gaby a lesson by arranging for the premiere of *The Belle of Bond Street* to take place at New Haven's Hyperion Theatre. This time the consequences were worse than before, for those on stage and for the audience. The Yale University students had not forgotten Gaby's last appearance here, and as soon as she walked on to the stage she was pelted with rotten eggs and tomatoes. Though her costume was ruined, she managed to finish her opening number before rushing off in tears, while Harry called the police and the stage-hands locked the theatre doors so that no one could get out. The ringleaders were arrested—two were identified from the previous incident, and ended up in jail.

The Belle of Bond Street opened at the Shubert Theatre on 30 May, and played to packed houses for 48 performances. Gaby and Harry had three song-and-dance sequences: *The Tango Dip, They Say I'm Frivolous* and *My Turkey-Trotting Boy*, while Harry's show-stopper was *Prunella*—forgotten today save by hard-core Broadway enthusiasts. It was Sam Bernard who received the most plaudits from the critics, while *Variety*'s much-hated Alan Dale denounced Gaby and Harry's routines as "lavatorial tornadoes". This time is was Bernard who left everyone in the lurch, when Famous Players' Adolf Zukor offered him a staggering $10,000 to appear in his first film, *Poor Schmaltz*. No sooner had Jake Shubert got over the shock of this than Zukor approached Gaby and offered her a contract for the same amount—which she promptly turned down. If Zukor could pay a "non-international" act like Sam Bernard $10,000, she argued, then he should pay *her* considerably more! Her nerve paid off. Zukor offered her $15,000 for a single film, and five per cent of the net receipts—and *still* Gaby made more demands. Firstly, Harry would be her leading man. Secondly, as she had no intention of ever returning to the United States, the film would be shot in Paris. Zukor agreed. On 22 May, Gaby and Harry boarded the *Imperator*.

Aboard the *Mauritania*,
glaring at photographers.

Evelyn Nesbit, who pestered Harry for sex…and Eva Tanguay, who threatened to "rearrange" his face!

Gaby in *The Little Parisienne*.

8: Stars of the Silent Screen

Nothing has survived of Gaby and Harry's first film, or of the short which preceded it. The short, *La remplaçant*, may have been a test-run for the film. Directed by René Hervil (1881-1960), it also featured Jean Angelo, who had recently appeared with Mistinguett in *Les Misérables*. Harry's name does not appear in the cast-list, but bearing in mind Gaby's insistence that he should be her co-star, otherwise there would *be* no film, one assumes he was in the production. The film's original title was *The Triumph*. And Gaby knew how to blow her own trumpet, when asked about her new venture. In America, *Motion Picture World* reported:

> Gaby Deslys before sailing was very enthusiastic over her first film engagement. She was certain it would develop into one of the greatest features ever conceived for the screen. According to reports from London, Gaby is making unprecedented efforts to contribute her share to bring about this result.

And in Britain, *Pictures & Picturegoer* observed:

> Few indeed have not heard of beautiful Gaby Deslys, whose fame has been made on the boards of the leading variety theatres of two Continents…Miss Deslys is noted, of course, for the wonderful and original gowns—many of great daring—in which she loves to appear, and in this connection she is said to have declared at a supper, "I myself like gowns that are a little daring. If a girl is beautiful, let her display her beauty to advantage. That makes the world happier. It is also good for the girl's future. I know a very pretty girl who came down to dinner

> dressed for a dance one evening in a very daring gown. But she was a beautiful girl—she had a beautiful figure—and so why complain? But the girl's father looked her up and down and then said bitterly, "Your mother never dressed like that to trap the men." "I know, father," said the girl, as she pinned a flower in her corsage, "And look at what she trapped!"

Gaby insisted that as the story was based on her rise to fame, *she* should write the script. Therefore there were the obligatory embellishments, not least of all that her character should have the same name. No one knows for sure who directed though one assumes this to have been René Hervil. The producer is listed as Daniel Frohman (1851-1940), who was Adolf Zukor's partner at Famous Players. Whether Hervil was actually in Paris for the five-day shoot is not known. Harry played Claude Devereux, but the names of the other actors are unknown. There were five reels and based on the available evidence the scenario is thus:

> Gaby is a poor music-hall understudy who, compelled to support her dying mother and blind sister, aspires for *vedette* status by making a play for the revue's leading man, Claude Devereux (Harry), who is involved in a stormy affair with his leading lady. In a fit of rage, the star gives the theatre manager an ultimatum: either Gaby goes, or she goes. The manager calls her bluff, and when she leaves he moves Gaby to the top of the bill and partners her with Claude. This results in the star taking a pot-shot at Gaby while she is taking her curtain-call. The bullet misses, so she has Gaby kidnapped by thugs, who are about to torture her in a country villa when Claude bursts in and rescues her, having been alerted by her blind sister,

who has overheard the abduction. All ends well when she collapses weeping into his arms.

The production had more than its share of problems. On the first day of shooting, Harry fell for one of the technicians—he moved out of Number Three, and into a hotel with his new lover. Accusing him of deserting her in her hour of need, Gaby threatened to walk off the set. The fact that Adolf Zukor had withheld $12,000 of her $15,000 salary until the film was finished prevented this from happening, though by the completion of the second reel she and Harry were no longer talking and when the camera-man tried to intervene, Harry threatened to thump him. Gaby then cabled Zukor and told him that, in view of her surviving the on-set squabbles, the film should be retitled *Her Triumph*. Zukor obliged.

Most contemporary reviews for the film have disappeared. A curious one appeared in a New Zealand regional newspaper the following year, and is included here exactly as published:

> The wonderful Parisian Dancer, whose charms cost a King his Throne, Gaby Deslys, appears for the first time on the screen in HER TRIUMPH, A DRAMA OF THE STAGE! LADIES! You simply must see Gaby's Hats and Frocks. Remember, she has been quoted as the world's fashion plate. MEN! Gaby is a charmer, and you can see her in two greatest dance creations, DANCE DESLYS and DANCE DES APACHES in which she is assisted by her partner HARRY PILCER, A Dancer of International Fame. The "Dance Deslys" is given at a fashionable reception before a distinguished social gathering, and is positively a remarkable exposition of terpsichorean skill. THE GOWNS & HEADGEAR are an amazing spectacle

to the gaze of mere man, but seen through the eyes of the fair sex they may be described as a VERITABLE ENCHANTMENT. GABY DESLYS also wears a necklet of pearls said to be worth a king's ransom. THE DANCES are not mere interpolations, but are appropriately wedded to the delightful drama. The great fame of GABY DESLYS is world-wide. It rings throughout Europe, Asia, Africa, and America, even to the smallest and remotest village of the Antipodes. Any attempt to describe the manifold charms and flashes of genius displayed by GABY DESLYS in "HER TRIUMPH" would be to "gild refined gold". Many tempting offers were made to GABY DESLYS to induce her to come to Australia and New Zealand, but all have failed. Her booked engagements in the Theatre of Paris, London, and New York date for more than three years ahead.

Gaby and Harry were still giving one another the cold shoulder when shooting wrapped, and on 14 July they were invited to a Bastille Day party at the film star Max Linder's home on the outskirts of Paris. Matters were not helped by the presence of the composer and occasional songwriter Reynaldo Hahn. Born in Venezuela in 1874, he studied under Massenet and by the turn of the century emerged as one of the most popular composers in France. In 1912, Sergei Diaghilev commissioned him and Jean Cocteau to score the ballet *Le dieu bleu*, but even when performed by the Ballets Russes this was a flop, and for a while Hahn concentrated on writing café-concert songs. One, *Voulez-vous, mon amour charmant*, was performed by Gaby but was written out of his unrequited love for Harry Pilcer:

> Voulez-vous, mon amour charmant,

> Que je vous épluche une orange?
> Vous avez des cils étonnants,
> Plus longs que les cheveux des anges!

> (My charming love,
> Would you like me to peel you an orange?
> You have astonishing eye-lashes,
> Longer than angels' hair!)

Besides Cocteau and Diaghilev, Hahn's long string of lovers included Marcel Proust and the composer Camille Saint-Saens. Harry almost certainly would have been added to the roster had his attempts at seduction not been thwarted by the incident at Max Linder's party which almost ended in tragedy. After dinner and an impromptu performance of *The Gaby Glide*, Linder and his guests went to watch a fireworks display taking place on the bank of the river flowing past the bottom of his garden. Around twenty people, including Gaby, were standing on the landing stage when the structure collapsed, flinging everyone into the water. Though a strong swimmer, Gaby was dragged along by the current because at the last moment—feeling cold even in July—she had put on a thick fur cloak. Harry acted instinctively, ripping off his clothes and diving into the river to save her. He drove her back to Paris, semi-conscious, and installed her in her bedroom at Number Three. The next morning she developed a chill which her doctor warned could turn into pneumonia unless she received proper care. When her mother arrived, Harry sent her packing, declaring that Gaby was *his* responsibility from now on. For a week he refused to leave her bedside. She pulled through, she later said, because he had whispered time and time again that he still loved her. This may or may not have been true—he certainly called his technician lover and told him that their relationship was over.

In the third week of July, Gaby and Harry headed to London, where they spent several days with Alfred Butt making the final arrangements for their next season at the Palace. The American musical-comedy star Elsie Janis (1899-1956) had proved the hit of the year in Arthur Wimperis's *The Passing Show*, and had signed a contract with the Shuberts to take this to Broadway. Appearing with her would be another Elsie—Harry's sister. Butt was hoping that Gaby would replace Janis, but she refused to work in any show that had not been commissioned exclusively for her. The director hired Wimperis to write a five-scene burlesque, which Gaby decided should be called *The Rajah's Ruby*. The premiere was pencilled in for the spring of 1915, and Gaby and Harry left for Paris to set about organising the costumes. On 2 August, Harry took her to Ostend for a short break, thinking that the sea air would benefit her health. They shared a hotel room, and their attempted reconciliation might have proved successful had it not been for the news, two days later, that war had been declared.

Harry decided that, despite his immigrant status, he would volunteer for military service. Gaby tried to talk him out of it by saying he was too old—he was only twenty-nine—but this only made him more determined to enlist. The situation was saved by a visit from Gaby's doctor, who broke the news, in the wake of recent tests, that she was in the early stages of consumption. Harry opted not to tell her, and risk her having a relapse.

A few days later, Gaby asked Harry to accompany her to London. The premiere of *The Rajah's Ruby* had been brought forward to 21 September, but she insisted that this was not the reason for the visit. Harry booked passages on the overnight steamer to Dover. They were met in London not by Alfred Butt, but by Mariano Unzué, who it emerged had met Gaby secretly during their last trip to the city. He and Harry almost came to blows, until the Argentinian revealed that Gaby had given him the task of finding her a house. There was just one stipulation. The house was to be in Kensington, and as near as possible to J. M. Barrie's apartment! Harry told Gaby that if this happened, he would be on the first ship back to New York, and she would never see him again. His opinion, that Barrie was a child molester, would never change.

The Rajah's Ruby shared the Palace bill with *The Passing Show*, with Florence Sweetman taking over from Elsie Janis. Billed as "A Burglarious Melo-drama", the critics hailed it Gaby's best show so far. She interpreted the role of Liane de Fleurs, a friend of the jewel thief Arsene Lupin (Harry) who dreams of becoming involved with the equally notorious Raffles, whose quest is to steal the priceless rajah's ruby from a dotty old baron (Arthur Playfair) whom she eventually marries. Playing Raffles was Basil Hallam (1889-1916), Elsie Janis' lover whose theme-song, *Gilbert The Filbert*, was included in every show he appeared in, inasmuch as Gaby and Harry performed *The Gaby Glide* almost every time they stepped on to a stage.

The backstage fights with Harry took a toll on Gaby's health, though she exacerbated these by secretly negotiating with Alfred Butt for an increase in her salary but not Harry's. When he found out what she had been up to, he told her that, on account of her greed, this revue would be their last. For the time being, she was unperturbed. She had also without his knowledge signed the contract for her next revue, with or without him, to open in the spring of 1915. Additionally, J. M. Barrie had placed his story, *Rosy Rapture*, in the hands of the scriptwriters. There was also another potential lover, another Harry, waiting in the wings—Harry Gordon Selfridge, the founder of London's famous society store, and twenty-five years her senior.

According to Captain Alastair Mackintosh, who wrote about his friendship with Basil Hallam in his memoirs, there was a nasty embarrassing confrontation in Gaby's dressing-room, after the premiere:

> Harry came in whilst I was talking to her. He was very excitable having apparently just discovered her earnings, which in those days were the highest paid to any artist save an operatic star. "It's not fair," he protested, pacing up and down. "It's just not fair that you should be getting five-hundred and fifty pounds a week, and I only fifty. You ought to give me some of it, Gaby. After all, I made you!" She swung round from her dressing-table and, hurling a scalding French epithet at him, added furiously, "*You* didn't make me…the King of Portugal made me!"

Mackintosh adds that Hallam, never less than the perfect gentleman, made a futile attempt to prevent the quarrel from getting out of hand. Another source stated that he retreated to avoid being hit by Harry, whom he hated "more than any man on earth". The reason for this resentment was brought into the open a few months later when Hallam was called up to fight. He confessed to a fellow soldier that despite living with Elsie Janis, he had been madly in love with Gaby, but afraid to express his feelings. In August 1916, aged twenty-seven, he was killed in the Battle of the Somme, and when Gaby received news of his death, she sent money to his family.

The playbill for the lost film, *Her Triumph*.

A publicity still for *Her Triumph*.

Gaby and Harry in *Her Triumph*…

…and with Basil Hallam.

9: The Great War

Harry Gordon Selfridge was born in 1858 in Ripon, Wisconsin, and raised by a domineering but caring mother after his father was killed in the American Civil War. At fourteen he began working in a bank, and at twenty-five changed direction and took a position as retail manager of Marshall Fields, then the largest department store in Chicago. He later became a partner, and his tactical business brain earned him the nickname "Mile-a-Minute-Harry" enabling the company to open branches right across the country. In 1890 he married wealthy heiress Rose Buckingham. He remained with Marshall Fields until 1904 when he set up a business of his own. Two years later, on a trip to London with his wife, he saw great potential should they open a store here, and invested over £400,000 in the project. Selfridges opened in March 1909 in a blaze of publicity and earned Selfridge another moniker, "The Earl of Oxford Street".

Selfridge was a serial adulterer, and was particularly fond of exotic dancers—his conquests included both Dolly Sisters, Anna Pavlova and Isadora Duncan. Though some have cited Gaby as having been the great love of his life, their relationship was one-sided. Despite their constant fights, when she met Selfridge she was still in love with Harry Pilcer, and would still be madly in love with him when Selfridge was out of the picture.

The Rajah's Ruby broke off for the Christmas holidays, and after the last performance Gaby complained to Harry of feeling unwell. Thinking this was a ruse to lure him back into her arms, he left for his hotel. Selfridge audaciously took her back to his house, and incredibly his wife put her to bed. During the night she developed a temperature, and a throat specialist was summoned. He diagnosed a small malignant growth on her vocal cords and on

Christmas Eve she underwent an emergency operation, which she barely survived. Harry, holding himself responsible for what had happened, spent most of Christmas Day at the hospital, but left when a huge basket of lilies arrived from Selfridge. The next morning she received a visit from Alfred Butt, who callously informed her that he had replaced her in *The Rajah's Ruby* with San Francisco-born Ethel Levey, former wife of the showman, George M. Cohan. She next received word that Harry was to appear in his own revue at the London Pavilion with Argentinian musical-comedy star Teddie Gerard (Teresa Cabre, 1890-1942), with whom he had worked briefly in Chicago in 1909. This was not him being revengeful, as the press reported—he needed the money to offer Gaby the best medical care possible.

Gaby jumped to the wrong conclusion about Harry. Incensed and hardly capable of standing on her feet, she discharged herself from the hospital and left for Marseille, where Anna Caire was nursing her sick husband. It is not known what sort of reception Hippolyte offered his errant daughter, though doubtless the money she gave him made up for any dissention there might have been between them. While she was here, she received a call from Mariano Unzué, announcing he had found her the perfect house in Kensington and that Gordon Selfridge—whom she had not even bothered to say goodbye to—had secured a long lease on the property for £4,000. Gaby sent him a letter promising that she would pay him back. She never did.

Harry rented a small apartment off Shaftesbury Avenue. He then jumped out of the frying pan into the fire when he began rehearsing with Teddie Gerard. When they had worked together in Chicago, she had been just eighteen, demure, and married to the theatrical agent, Joseph Raymond. Now, she had left him, and heavy drinking had transformed her into a spitfire ten times worse than Gaby had ever been. She loathed homosexuals and frequently lashed out at the young men hanging around the stage door every evening in the hope of catching a glimpse of the handsome Harry—and, if they were lucky, being invited back to his flat for a little fun. As Harry had always despised drunken women, it was inevitable that there would be problems.

Teddie Gerard attempted to cure Harry of his "affliction" by coercing him into visiting her hotel room and, after hitting him over the head and rendering him semi-conscious, she ripped off his clothes and, when he came around tried to force him to have sex with her. Her idea was that as Gaby Deslys had an Argentinian lover—Mariano—then Harry should have one too. He reacted by slapping her around before throwing her out, though some good did come out of the situation when he incorporated what had happened, with little censorship, into their act when they opened in *The Butterfly* on 4 January 1915 at the London Pavilion.

The revue's reception was mixed, with the critics variously hailing it "sensationally brilliant", "provocative", or "copiously vulgar". Many people stormed out of the theatre during the final sketch when Teddie Gerard flung Harry backwards over a trunk before renting his shirt in two—after which he remained spread-eagled across this, his long hair almost sweeping the boards, for several minutes while this "butterfly" flitted around him, pausing every now and then—in Gerard's own words—to "suck nectar" from his nipples and navel! And if Harry seemed to enjoy being dominated by this man-hungry woman, he is said to have hated every moment he spent on the stage with her, and "rued the day" that he had agreed to a clause in his contract that there would be a follow-up revue with her after this one. The fact that he was earning over £1,000 a week prevented him from throwing in the towel and heading back to New York.

Gaby's return to London in the first week of February went unnoticed by the press. At once, she threw herself into rehearsals for the new J. M. Barrie revue, *Rosy Rapture: The Pride of the Beauty Chorus*, scheduled to open at the Duke of York's Theatre on 22 March. She moved into her new house at 13 Kensington Gore, a smart Georgian property opposite the Royal Albert Hall, which offered a splendid view across Hyde Park. Superstitious about the number, she changed it to 12a, and a few weeks later held an open-day for the press. The expensive furnishings were paid for by Harry Gordon Selfridge and J. M. Barrie, the latter at a low edge because his lover George du Maurier and his foster son George Llewellyn Davies had left to fight at the Front. The *Sketch*, dated 14 April 1915, depicted Gaby "relaxing" in each room of the house in staged poses, each photograph given a caption which gullible admirers believed really had been penned by her:

> Good day! You see, I greet my favourite paper in my favourite room…it is all Turkish!

> Of course I like playing in *Rosy Rapture*! Who would *not* love to be in a Barrie burlesque?

> I don't feel like the Pride of the Beauty Chorus when I am at the piano. I take my music seriously!

> London often makes me think of Paris, darling. Even its spring weather is like ours…sometimes!

The bedroom at Kensington Gore was the focal point of Gaby's home and way over the top even by her standards. She called it her shrine, and it was exactly this. Even Harry, during their many reconciliations, was terrified of sleeping there. In an alcove, set upon a dais reached by several steps, was an ornate, gilded four-poster, its canopy supported by a pair of golden cherubs. Behind this structure was a pair of velvet curtains which, when opened, revealed a stained-glass window in front of which was an elaborate crucifix. The effect of this resulted in a "heavenly" glow which filled the room even in daylight hours. To one side, within a cusped cabinet, was a life-sized Madonna encircled by votive candles which Gaby kept lit at all times. Elsewhere, there were chinchilla rugs, priceless statues and works of art.

On 21 March, the dress-rehearsal of *Rosy Rapture* was filmed, and the single reel used to promote the revue in London cinemas. Directed for the Neptune Film Company by Percy Nash (1868-1958), who later directed the original *Hobson's Choice*, it was scripted by J. M. Barrie, and besides Gaby featured Biddy de Burgh and John East, while there were guest appearances by G. K. Chesterton and George Bernard Shaw. That same day, Gaby learned of the death in action of Barrie's lover, Guy du Maurier, on 9 March. When she rushed around to Adelphi Terrace to console her friend, however, she was told that he was too upset to see even her. The next morning, word came from Flanders that Barrie's twenty-one-year-old foster son had also been killed, six days after du Maurier. Barrie's grief was so intense that he did not attend Gaby's premiere.

Rosy Rapture was the only London production where Gaby played to empty seats, though this was not her fault. It was staged as part of a double bill with Barrie's stark one-act play, *The New Word*. Subtitled *A Fireside Scene,* this told of a working-class family's involvement with the war, and critics were undecided whether the author was being patriotic, or merely profiteering from the conflict. A large part of the first-night audience were soldiers on leave from the Front, and despite their admiration for Gaby were in no frame of mind to be reminded of the horrors they had left behind on the battlefields of Flanders. When she walked on to the stage, even to a rowdy ovation, her task of cheering the audience cannot have been easy. Even two songs by the then little-known Jerome Kern did not help and an unexplained seven-minute interval between two of the scenes robbed the piece of its continuity. Gaby also had problems with her dancing partner Jules Raucourt, whom she serenaded in near incomprehensible English with Kern's *When I Discover My Man*:

> It's not flirting, you'll agree,
> That makes me change my mind to love just one man, then another.
> Then I merely try to find the one man worth all the bother.
> I would not marry Tom or Dick…or Harry!

The emphasis on "Harry" became a topic of conversation with Gaby's critics, unsure which Harry she was referring to—Pilcer or Selfridge. Raucourt, a tetchy Belgian, tried to convince her that if *he* became her lover, she would forget both. Gaby was not interested, and announced that she was no longer interested in love, but in furthering her career and earning as much money as she could—not for herself, but to aid the loved ones of her countrymen killed in the war. She was already donating half of her salary to the French Relief Fund, and it is a pity that this was ignored by the media, particularly by the reporter writing for *The Times* on 23 March:

> Apparently, Miss Deslys is an institution. She must be nothing less to have a revue written for her, on purpose, by Sir James Barrie. As soon as you set eyes on her you know it; you can see it in her gait, in her daring costumes and her daring semi-nudes, in the way she takes the stage, in her whole behaviour. She can dance you any dance: the dance graceful and *legato*, the dance comic and staccato,

the dance epileptic and frenzied. It is here that she is really rapturous, with the joy of the artist in creating art. Further, she is an everlasting high-pressure source of energy, never at rest and, as people say, all over the place...You are fascinated by her dancing, repelled by something macabre about her, enlivened and in the end rather fatigued by her enormous energy...No doubt, for special tastes Miss Deslys offers special provocations. The devotees of dress must worship her. Amateurs of bare backs must find her priceless. English people who like to have their language tortured out of recognition must revel in her. But in the end you have to come back to the old view: she is a theme for dinner-table and smoking-room gossip. And now her talent has been hallmarked "J.M.B." in the corner! We wish we could recognize the process as reciprocal; we wish "G.D." in the corner could hallmark Sir James' talent. To be frank, it does not. If it were not for the name on the playbill and some mechanical jokes on the stage, we would never have detected Sir James' hand in this revue...but it all comes back in the end to the institution, to Miss Deslys and her wonderful dances, and her wonderful dresses, and her rather sick smile, and her incomprehensible jargon, and her celebrated expanse of bare back. If you are more attracted than repelled by her you will be more pleased than bored by *Rosy Rapture*.

Reading this and other scurrilous articles about the revue, biased and exaggerated, brought Barrie out of his depression, and he realised that unless he took positive action, both *Rosy Rapture* and *The New Word* faced early closure. Gaby was unperturbed, aware that if one revue closed, she would be offered another. Barrie cabled his friend, Charles Frohman, in New York. It was he who had promoted the stage version of *Peter Pan* in 1904, and he was about to make his annual trip to London. Barrie was sure that Frohman would come up with fresh ideas. On 1 May 1915, the producer boarded the British liner *Lusitania*. Six days later, within sight of the Irish coastline, the vessel was hit by two torpedoes fired by the German U-boat, *U-20*, and sank at once. Of the 1,962 passengers and crew, 1,198 lost their lives—124 of them Americans, including Frohman. For the third time in as many months Barrie was plunged into deepest mourning, and on 29 May as a result of him losing all interest in his work, both revues closed.

The press had a field-day. Scoops about Barrie's "unusual" private life filled entire pages, even in other-wise conservative publications such as *The Tatler*. References were made to his "intricate" friendship with Antarctic explorer Robert Falcon Scott in an article headed, "How Gaby Went From Harry To Barrie, And Harry Went From Gaby To Teddie, And Then How Gaby, Who Had Gone From Harry To Barrie, Went Back To Harry Again!"

Gaby returned to Kensington Gore, where there were press-conferences, and garden-parties thrown to aid wounded soldiers, and at which she delivered quaint speeches and promises of more money to assist the war-effort, which she would keep. Matichon came over from Paris for a visit. Harry, welcomed back into the fold now that his second revue with Teddie Gerard had been cancelled, escorted them around London. Cecil Beaton, eleven years old at the time, recalled meeting her and praised her beyond recognition in *The Book of Beauty* (1930). In 1954, in *The Glass of Fashion*, he was still drooling over the "magenta" woman:

> Magenta orchids trembled at her breast. Magenta were her lace stockings, and her shoes were of magenta satin with magenta ribbons criss-crossed up her legs. Pale magenta cheeks and lips had been painted on a face the colour of

marshmallow. Vulgar, perhaps…but by whose standards? The gesture seemed to transcend vulgarity and create its own allure.

Gaby's next project was the only one of her London revues *not* written with her in mind. André Charlot, her former agent who had been instrumental in introducing her to the Shuberts, had taken over from Alfred Moul as manager of the Alhambra Theatre in 1912. Back in January, aware of the content of J. M. Barrie's *The New Word*, he had begun preparing a revue which, he declared, would bear no references whatsoever to the horrors of the war. He advertised for chorus girls, and six-hundred turned up for the auditions for a line-up of sixteen. The provisional title was *1915*, but after having second thoughts Charlot announced that a prize of five guineas would go to whoever came up with the best title, in no more than four words, and one which must *not* refer to the war. The winner, proposed by a staff member at the Alhambra, was *5064 Gerrard*. The revue opened on 19 March.

Charlot asked Gaby to augment the production, only to have her denounce the title as a sick joke put forward by Harry, whom she accused of dumping her to take up with *Teddie* Gerard. In fact, *5064 Gerrard* was the telephone number of the theatre! While audiences had dwindled for Gaby's revue, this had played to full houses since the premiere. Its stars represented the most dazzling array of collective talent the city had seen in years and included rising American star Beatrice Lillie (1894-1989) in her first London production, Australian funnyman-dancer Clyde Cook (1891-1984), and Robert Hale (1874-1940), perhaps the greatest comedian of his day. Hale excelled in a sketch entitled "The Terrible Trial", which had audiences splitting their sides with laughter. In it he played an ugly overgrown female child prodigy, and the caption referring to this in the programme declared, "The revolving stage patented by the Alhambra will support the weight of the entire company, including the celebrated child actress!" Another sketch entitled "At Murray's Club" alluded to the nightclub on Beal Street where Harry and Teddie Gerard had danced the Tango on their evenings off from *Butterfly*. Hale interpreted the role of "Miss Rosy Rapture" which of course alluded to Gaby. Wearing a long flimsy gown, voile headdress and several strings of over-sized pearls he crooned "Frenchie-Scottie" to Clyde Cook, who was dressed in a tartan kilt and balding wig. James Barrie was outraged at the caricature. So too was Gaby, who nevertheless decided to use it to her advantage when Charlot finally persuaded her to join the cast the day after *Rosy Rapture* closed.

On 31 May, Gaby held a press-conference at Kensington Gore, where Charlot presented her with the revised script, which he told the gathering had been overhauled "to accommodate her diverse talents". She flicked through this, announced that she would be free to join the revue on 3 June—then she announced "two teensy little changes" that she had made of her own, providing these met with Charlot's approval. He nodded, hardly aware of what he was letting himself in for. Firstly, she said, one of her chihuahas would appear in a sketch. Charlot was fine with this. Secondly, the "flirty and arrogant" Jules Raucourt would *not* be partnering her. Harry Pilcer would! And while Charlot was staring open-mouthed at this, Gaby offered a compromise. *Unless* he hired Harry as her leading man, she would be returning to Paris on 2 June, instead of going to the theatre for the dress-rehearsal! Publicly forced into a tight corner, Charlot had no option but to submit to her demands.

Because things had progressed so fast, there was insufficient time to add Gaby and Harry's names to the programmes and posters, therefore the public had no idea when they would make their entrance in the revue—or if they would appear at all, and whether the announcement in the press that morning had been just a gimmick to sell tickets now that sales had begun to dip. Gaby came on during Robert Hale's impersonation of her, crying above the frenzied applause, "Well, which one of us do you think is the *real* Gaby Deslys?" The audience roared their appreciation—more so when Harry strode on and they danced *The Gaby Glide*. In another sketch, Gaby appeared with Beatrice Lillie, who sang *I Want To Go Back To Michigan* dressed as a bumbling farm labourer—proving so popular that for years she would be offered only butch roles.

Gaby and Harry's other sketches raised the roof, proving them excellent comedians in their own right. In *Saint Pancras*, Harry has had a nervous breakdown on account of Gaby's "over-demanding charm" and been told by his doctor not to see her for a week. He has changed his name to St Pancras and taken refuge in his bachelor quarters in the country. Gaby happens to be driving past when her car runs out of petrol. She enters the building, but neither recognizes the other because they are wearing disguises. What follows was Gaby parodying herself with her bad English:

GABY: Oh-la-la! What shall I do? The flying bedstead has come off the handle and I am fainted!
HARRY: There, there! We can easily get a spare one to fit the handle!
GABY: I can afford to lose the Ford, but I must find my Harry!
HARRY: Harry? Harry Barry?
GABY: No, Harry 'Arry! My Harry has run away. He calls himself Saint Julian. That's one-shilling a half-bottle. Touch me not!
HARRY: What's he like?
GABY: He's like you, only he has longer hair and speaks with a Scotch accent!

The revised *At Murray's Club* sketch, this time with the real Gaby and Harry, was more hilarious than the original. It began with Harry and his friend (Jack Morrison) discussing Gaby, whom neither has met. Harry has sent her a letter asking her to supper, and she has agreed to meet him because he signed himself "The Champion Dancer of America. He gets a shock when *two* Gabys enter from opposite sides of the stage, wearing identical dresses. And of course, he is unable to distinguish the real Gaby from Robert Hale in drag. There follows a quick-fire exchange of dialogue, a mixture of French and English mala-propisms which audiences must have found almost impossible to comprehend. One line caused Harry's previous partner great offence—this was when Hale kissed him and pronounced, "What a nice boy you are. You remind me of Teddie Gerard!" This was subsequently replaced with the name "Ted Sloan", which was even worse—this was Gerard's nick-name on account of her fondness for getting drunk on Sloan Rangers cocktails! The song following this repartee, after the two Gabys had a tug of war and pulled Harry's arms off, was their send-up of Harry Lauder's *I Love A Lassie*:

> Loosh! Ye'll turn the Highland fling into a skittish reel!
> I shall simply smile and fling my clothes away, piecemeal!
> Oh how J. M. Barrassing,
> When I and my friend Harry sing,
> We don't like too much on…
> I love a Barrie, he's nicer far than Harry,
> And I'll teach him The Gaby Glide as well!
> We'll dance it together,
> So stop your tickling, Jimmy!
> Don't' be shy, come along and have a try,
> With Gaby our French Blue Belle!

Gaby's chihuahua did not appear in the revue. On the eve of the premiere he was stolen from her dressing-room. Trailed by reporters, she went to Scotland Yard and reported the theft. "I am offering a reward of twenty pounds for my little Bébé's speedy return," she announced on the steps of the building. "I've heard that they eat little dogs like him in China!" Three weeks into the run the dog was found safe and well, and there were suggestions that it had all been a publicity stunt, and that the dog had never been kidnapped in the first place. What followed was not. To celebrate Bébé's return, Gaby took the entire company out to dine at one of London's most exclusive restaurants, and while here was incensed to hear a group of society toffs cracking jokes about the war. The next day, she decided that she would have to concentrate *entirely* on raising funds for wounded soldiers, and for the families of those who had lost loved ones and were struggling to survive— that to do this, she would have to leave *5064 Gerrard* and take her show on the road. It would be the first time she had ever performed outside London, and of course, she would be taking her partner with her.

Harry was delighted. For two years he had been trying to enlist, without avail, and felt guilty about not "doing his bit". Now, he could. Despite the cruel jibes about his homosexuality— something he made no attempt at hiding, besides which he still travelled everywhere with his "lucky" teddy-bear—he was no coward. The couple left the revue at the end of June, and were offered a tour by the Moss Empire to begin at the end of July. Work commitments had resulted in them missing the London premiere of *Her Triumph* but it was scheduled to open nationally as a staggered release so that they could attend a gala first night each time they arrived in a new town or city. For six weeks, they worked around the clock, catching a few hours' sleep here and there, and despite the warnings from Gaby's doctors that she was not up to it. Gaby was paid £1,500 a week and Harry £1,000—a phenomenal sum in the days when the average weekly wage was around £1, though once they had taken out their expenses they gave the rest to charity. Prior to the tour, Harry visited convalescent homes in and around London, giving lessons in exercise and physiotherapy. Gaby went into hospitals where she assisted the nurses, gave out food parcels, and raffled some of her clothes to raise money for the wives and mothers of soldiers who had died there since returning from the Front. When one wounded soldier told her that he could not wait to get back on his motorcycle, she had one brought around to the hospital and took him for a ride down Oxford street—she driving, and him in the sidecar.

Régine Flory was in town, appearing in a revue at the Empire Theatre, and on 15 July she and Gaby joined forces for a French Flag Day parade which raised hundreds of pounds for the war effort and finished up outside 10 Downing Street. Next morning the two women, who became close friends, travelled to Brighton to begin a tour of convalescent homes and hospitals. It was a scorching hot day, but Gaby still wore her favourite chinchilla coat while riding a donkey along the beach—before mingling with the crowd of onlookers with a bucket, collecting funds. To cheer those still fighting she arranged for parcels of her photographs to be sent to the Front. As such, she became the first pin-up of the war—while more than a few soldiers had "Vienna" pictures of a scantily-clad Harry tucked inside their knapsacks. More importantly Gaby wired Mariano Unzué—in Buenos Aires on a business trip, though he would soon return to Arlette Dorgère at their Vigneux-sur-Seine chateau—and arranged for Britain's very first importation of tinned corned-beef. This was sent into France by the ton, and when news of Gaby's charitable activities reached the French government, President Poincaré awarded her the prestigious *Caporal d'Honneur*.

Gordon Harry Selfridge

J. M. Barrie

Teddie Gerard.

10: *Stop! Look! Listen!*

Little is known of the first Deslys-Pilcer tour. There was an embarrassing incident when they played the Queen's Hotel in Harrogate. After the show they were introduced to their guest-of-honour—Princess Augusta Victoria, consort of the deposed Manuel of Portugal! Though Harry acted with his usual charm and diplomacy, Gaby (according to Régine Flory) refused to curtsy, telling Augusta to her face that she had only had Manuel's cock inside her after Gaby Deslys had decided not to have it inside *her* any more! And when the young princess reprimanded her for her "surprisingly unladylike behaviour", Gaby retorted, "Why *should* I curtsy to you? You're not a *real* queen. I'm more of a queen than you'll ever be—the queen of the music-hall!"

The tour ended in Newcastle at the end of September, when Gaby was contacted by Charles Dillingham, who had worked with Harry. He had seen her in *Her Triumph*, and was of the opinion that she could act as well as just parade around in fancy clothes. He was planning a new revue, scored by a newish young songwriter called Irving Berlin, and wanted her to take it on a 30-weeks tour of America. Their previous collaboration, *Watch Your Step*, had taken Broadway by storm, created for Vernon and Irene Castle, who would one day take over from where Gaby and Harry left off. Initially, Gaby was reluctant to accept. She had been fêted in America, but she had also been ridiculed and insulted, not just in New Haven, but by the press and by Jake Shubert. Harry got her to change her mind, and she cabled Dillingham to announce that she—and Harry—would be delighted to work for him. The couple headed for Paris to organise their costumes and make the travel arrangements. Because passages were restricted on account of the war, they crossed the Channel in a military vessel.

If the couple's arrival in Paris went unnoticed by the press, their departure from Le Havre during the last week of October did not. Harry wore a brightly-coloured suit and clutched his ubiquitous teddy-bear. Gaby, wearing her chinchilla coat, posed for photographs with one of her Chihuahuas—she and the dog were wearing matching earrings with pearls the size of sparrows' eggs. One of the reporters took time to count her trunks as they were being loaded on to the steamer—180 of them.

Stop! Look! Listen! premiered in Philadelphia on 1 December 1915 to a frantic reception. Besides Gaby and Harry there was Harry Fox, with whom they had worked before, and Marion Davies (1897-1961), who the following year became the long term mistress of newspaper magnate William Randolph Hearst. It was Fox who had the big production number, perhaps the only one that is remembered today. Accompanied by Murray Pilcer's jazz-band, *I Love A Piano* saw him dancing ragtime across the keys of a huge grand piano which filled the entire stage. A particular thorn in Harry's side, bearing in mind that he choreographed the show, was Charles Dillingham's decision to partner Gaby not with him, but with Joseph Santley (1890-1971), who early on in the revue crooned *The Girl On The Magazine Cover* to Davies, in front of a *Vogue* cover backdrop. Then, realizing his mistake when the first-night audience started chanting Harry's name while Santley was crooning *I Love To Dance* to Gaby—wearing a seven-foot tall skyscraper hat!—Dillingham did some swapping around and Harry, aka Anthony St Anthony, replaced him in the sketch. The production closed with an extended Gaby and Harry sequence. He performed *I'll Be Coming Home With A Skate On*, then moved aside while she half-sung, half-spoke *Everything In America Is Ragtime*...which inevitably faded into *The Gaby Glide*.

The revue transferred to New York, where Gaby and Harry took up residence at the Savoy Hotel. It opened on Christmas Day at Broadway's Globe Theatre, where its fortune changed somewhat dramatically. *The New York Times* enthused:

> What an orgy of Ragtime! Miss Gaby-aby-aby-aby Deslys-elys-elys appears, at the request of Mr Charles Dilly-Dee Dillingham in a dozen breathtaking Parisian bathroom scenes while crooning songs such as *Take Off A Little Bit More* to the perfectly syncopated rhythm of ragtime!

In its 16 January 1916 issue, the theatre critic from *Green Book Magazine* praised Joseph Santley, Harry Fox and the "articulate" chorus girls, barely mentioned Harry, and made it clear that he did not care much for Gaby:

> Finally, to obey the implied injunction that the first shall be last, there is Gaby Deslys. Mr. Fox tells The Lady of the Lilies, "I think you're clever," and Mr. Fox is entitled to his opinion, but it isn't ours. To us, Mlle. Deslys always has seemed quite an ordinary French soubrette, full of gurgles, gasps and aspirations. Here, however, she does two rather remarkable dances—one with Mr. Santley and one with Harry Pilcer —and wears some astounding costumes, including a hat that looks as though its plumage had been lifted from a pink hearse.

Upon reading this, Charles Dillingham put Santley back into the *I Love To Dance* sequence, and moved Harry further down the bill. This led to a bust-up which saw Gaby taking the producer's side, and Harry throwing a tantrum and threatening to boycott the show. When Dillingham vowed to fire him before allowing this to happen, and when Gaby *still* supported Dillingham, Harry rubbed salt into her wounds by revealing that he had already entered into negotiations to form a new double-act with Teddie Gerard—currently appearing in an off-Broadway revue. These fell through when, after an afternoon matinee, Harry returned to his hotel room to find an inebriated, naked and very aggressive Gerard in his bed and was left with no alternative but to call the police, who arrested her for being drunk and disorderly.

The next morning, Harry went to see his friend, E. F. Albee (1857-1930) the former roustabout with P. T. Barnum who later co-founded RKO Pictures, and currently managing the Palace Theatre, on the corner of Broadway and Forty-Seventh Street. Albee had been wanting to book Harry for some time, but not with Gaby, whom he considered too profane for his audiences. He proposed a revue which would see Harry sharing the bill with singer-comedienne Nora Bayes, of *Shine On, Harvest Moon* fame. *Harry Pilcer Presents* would feature a sketch with Harry's sister, Elsie—parodying Gaby, who she disliked—with her dance-partner Dudley Douglas. This was scheduled to open at the end of March, though Harry was not sure he would be able to make the premiere, as he was still under contract to Charles Dillingham.

On New Year's Eve, meanwhile, there was a massive row between Gaby and Dillingham, when ahead of the performance he walked on the stage and told the audience that the next evening's show, a gala in collaboration with the Shuberts at the 5,300-seater Hippodrome Theatre on Sixth Avenue, would begin with Gaby presenting one of her diamond bracelets to the parents of the first baby girl born in New York in 1916. Gaby told the audience that this would not happen, adding that the entire cast of *Stop! Look! Listen!* had agreed to donate their salaries for the evening to her French Soldiers Fund, something which had been kept secret from Dillingham, whom she denounced as "stingy" for having earlier refused to donate to her charity.

The arguments between Gaby, Harry and Dillingham began affecting Gaby's performances—as yet she knew nothing about Harry's proposed Palace revue, otherwise matters would have been infinitely worse. She began fluffing her lines, and more than once rushed off the stage in tears when she missed a step while dancing. The much-hated Alan Dale observed in *Variety*, "What a great revue this would be with a *real* leading lady!" The crunch came when Harry told a reporter that he alone had been responsible for making Gaby a household name in America, which of course was true. Gaby threw one strop too many, and Dillingham announced that *Stop! Look! Listen!* would close on 25 March. This saw the couple rushing to their lawyers. Their contract with Dillingham still had over a month to run, and he was told to either put them into another show, or pay them the salaries they would have received, had the revue completed its season. Forced into a corner, Dillingham offered a compromise—the revue *would* continue, but at Boston's Colonial Theatre. Harry got in touch with E. F. Albee, and asked him to remove his sister Elsie's *Gaby* sketch from the forthcoming Palace bill, and not to use the title *Harry Pilcer Presents*, seeing as he would not now be in it. Albee refused, and Harry realised that he had gone *too* far when Gaby was shown Alan Dale's review of one of the rehearsals in *Variety*, shortly before going on stage one evening in Boston:

> The new Gaby Deslys has made her entrance through a wisteria hedge, wearing a hooped frock, and the most grotesquely huge head-dress.

Gaby later said that the month she spent in Boston was the most miserable period of her life. On 14 April, one hour before the penultimate performance of *Stop! Look! Listen!* she received a cable from her mother in Marseille, informing her that her father had died on 28 January. Why Anna Caire had taken so long to inform her is not known, or why Gaby became so upset when she had not been particularly close to the man who had practically disowned her. The audience was told that the show had been cancelled, but no one wanted to leave the theatre until they had seen Gaby. Harry coaxed her on to the stage, and she dedicated the show to Hippolyte's memory.

The next evening, Gaby was performing *Everything In America Is Ragtime*, and Harry was in the wings, waiting to whisk her into the show's finale, when he was informed that a lawyer was waiting for them in the manager's office, with a police officer. Gaby's former associate H. B. Marinelli had filed a claim stating that *he* had negotiated the contract with Charles Dillingham, and that the couple owed him a percentage of their salary, which would have to be paid tonight—if not, they would be arrested and thrown into jail! Harry joined her for the finale, muttered into her ear what had happened, and they incorporated their getaway into *The Gaby Glide*, rushing off the stage and along a succession of corridors, leaving the theatre via a door in the cellar while the audience were chanting for an encore. Less than an hour later, they boarded the night-train to New York. Her actions cost Gaby dearly. Charles Dillingham retained $6,000 of her salary—though curiously none of Harry's—as a "fine", and this was handed over to Marinelli. Gaby vowed never to set foot in America again, and this time stressed that she meant it.

There was a further crisis when the couple began making arrangements to return to France. America was yet to augment the conflict in Europe, and because his parents had been born there Harry was deemed "a suspicious alien" and his passport impounded. Additionally, Jake Shubert filed a suit against him for money he claimed he had lost when Harry had walked out of *The Honeymoon Express*. Gaby made several much-publicised visits to the French and English consulates, but her pleas fell on deaf ears. Harry advised her to leave without him and promised to follow her across the Atlantic as soon as he had acquired a visa. Her father's affairs were in a mess, and her mother and sister said to be near-destitute.

Her father's death, and her persistent ill-health brought about the drafting of Gaby's will, in her suite at the Savoy Hotel on the establishment's monogrammed writing paper on 29 April, which happened to be Harry's thirty-first birthday. The next morning, it was handed over to a lawyer. The first section was bizarre, to say the least:

> I wish to be embalmed and buried looking as beautiful as possible, and blessed by a priest. I want a doctor to open a vein to ensure that I'm dead when they bury me. I request a beautiful coffin, an image of the Virgin to be placed on my breast, also the crucifix and the two rings that I always wear. If I die at sea and my body is found, I wish to be transported immediately to Marseille. If I die in England and my family is not there, my best friend Selfridge must be contacted. He will arrange everything, but he need not read my will.

There was a reason for this last sentence, as the next clause observed:

> I bequeath Harry Pilcer my collection of cigarette cases, and everything within my bedroom at Kensington Gore.

Gaby's cigarette cases were of comparatively little value. The contents of her bedroom—antiques, priceless works of art—were worth £500,000, around £6 million in today's money, and this did not include the jewels she kept in drawers and cabinets, which she also wanted Harry to have. These jewels aside, almost everything had been given to her by Selfridge and J. M. Barrie, who she obviously did not regard in the same light as Harry, whether they were always squabbling or not!

Two days later, Gaby sailed for England—and Alan Dale celebrated her departure by penning a mock obituary in *Variety*:

> The Gaby Deslys boom lasted a surprisingly long time. Some day an enterprising statistician will make a compilation of various "newspaper booms" and the lengths of their lives…a kind of handbook for the aspiring ones. With the facts and figures relentlessly set forth, these boom-mongers will know their bearings. Miss Gabrielle of the Lilies was comfortably carried along for several years too many.

Hyppolyte Caire had been buried in the St-Pierre Cemetery. Gaby purchased the plots on either side of his grave, and paid for a white marble family tomb and mausoleum to be erected on the site for when her time came. She told a reporter, "My father and I never got along while he was alive, but after my death I would like to be laid to rest beside him." Less than four years later, she would be.

Matichon Caire had left the music-hall, and was residing in the city with her South American industrialist husband, Fernand-Oscar de Conill. Leaving her mother in her capable hands, Gaby headed back to London. "Gaby returns with the summer, the flowers and with other bright things," *The Sketch* observed. For several weeks she took a well-earned rest at Kensington Gore.

Gordon Selfridge and James Barrie visited daily—the latter escorted her to the Empire Theatre to see *Follow The Crowd*, Arthur Wimperis's adaptation of *Stop! Look! Listen!* At the end of

May, Harry arrived in London, having finally been granted a visa to leave New York. Within days, the work poured in. He and Gaby were offered a second nationwide tour by the Moss organization, to commence in August. André Charlot assigned them to a revue to open at the Alhambra in December. Then Gaby fell ill—little more than a common cold to begin with, though this quickly turned to pneumonia and she was bedridden for several weeks. Upon her recovery, when she was feeling up to it she threw garden parties at her home, and she and Harry charged phenomenal fees for opening fêtes—every penny of which went to her French Soldiers Fund. At one of these, held in the grounds of the Chelsea Hospital on behalf of the Actors' Orphanage, the sugar-lump that she had been given to put into her tea was placed in a silk purse and raffled, raising over £100! The tour, however, had to be amended as no one wished to risk Gaby travelling too far during a cold British winter. At the end of November, instead of opening at the Alhambra in a new show, Gaby and Harry assembled a selection of their best sketches and dance-routines, and toured London and the Home Counties. By the time this opened at Stratford's New Cross Theatre it had a title: *Mademoiselle Zuzu*. Gaby was paid £1,200 a week, Harry £1,000. The tour ended at Finsbury Park in January 1917.

On 7 March, *The Sketch Supplement* ran the curious headline "G. Is For Gaby! '*Saucy Suzette*' And Her Initial". The editorial explained that her dream had always been to own a theatre and stage the kind of revues where she would be taken seriously as an actress as opposed to being regarded as a sex symbol. Though this would not happen, she came close to achieving her goal by announcing that she had hired the Globe Theatre, off Shaftesbury Avenue, and that she and Harry would be appearing there *not* in a revue, but in a musical-comedy with a credible plot. The writers were Austen Hurgen and George Arthurs and supplying the music was former child prodigy Max Darewski (1894-1929), who had conducted his first symphony aged just nine. André Charlot was producing, and had chosen the title *Saucy Suzette*. Days after the *Sketch* feature, Gaby announced that the word "saucy" had been removed from the title, so that audiences would be made aware that she had ditched her *coquette* image once and for all.

What would be Gaby and Harry's last London revue, and with 255 performances offer them their longest run, was hailed by most critics as their finest. Everything was scripted and choreographed by them. They held auditions for the cast and chorus, and among the co-stars they engaged were 14-year-old Nora Swinburne and comedian Stanley Lupino whose daughter Ida, born the following year, later took Hollywood by storm. Another was a 27-year-old French actor named Jean Maréchal, who quickly became Harry's lover and moved into the apartment he had retained, just around the corner from the theatre.

Suzette opened on 29 March, when the guest-of-honour was 60-year-old Anna Caire, who stayed at Kensington Gore for the entire run. Parts of Suzette's story were not far-removed from events in Gaby's life. It begins at a Marseille convent school, where she dreams of wedding a handsome and needless to say wealthy young man. What she gets is an arranged marriage with an older, uncaring country farmer—played by Yvan Servais, whose command of the English language was no better than her own. They meet, and he tries to please her by offering her a roster of duties. These include grooming the horses, getting up at four in the morning to feed "all those darling little piggies", and toiling in the fields for nothing, enabling him to save money on wages by discharging his other farmhands. She escapes the drudgery and by a series of clever but not entirely plausible twists in the plot achieves world fame as a music-hall singer, giving her an excuse to wear the latest over-the-top haute-couture of the day and effect more costume changes than in any previous revue. "Jingle" quipped in the 18 April issue of *The Bystander*, "One fancies that if Gaby hadn't become distinguished as an actress, she might easily have won fame as a milliner."

Harry portrayed American ne'er-do-well Bobby Keith, who sneaks over the convent wall to woo Suzette when the other girls have gone to bed—the part based on Gaby's first lover, Ludo. He introduced a new dance, "The Cold-Water Rag", described by André Charlot as "a most remarkable exhibition of a drunken man trying with unusual energy to get upstairs to bed". Taking up the whole of the second act, and which saw Gaby and Harry rewarded with a standing ovation every performance, was *The Cat and the Canary*, which began with Gaby perched in a huge gilded cage, suspended from the rafters. *The Times*' critic observed:

> Mademoiselle Gaby Deslys is the same as ever. Her mouth is still as wide, and constantly open. Her English is still so "broken" as to save one the trouble of trying to understand it. And her dancing is still as vigorous, as wild-animal, as exciting as ever. With that clever dancer Harry Pilcer to help her, she achieves wonders of athletic display. Their most ambitious effort shows Mlle Deslys as a canary and Mr. Pilcer as a cat. Mr. Darewski's music strains itself to bursting whilst the cat kills the canary, and afterwards, stricken with remorse, sobs and scatters flowers over the yellow corpse. The audience seemed to enjoy this tragic episode enormously, and applauded with violence. The feeling of the house was on the whole against the two gallery gentlemen who in the first act expressed their estimate of the piece's value by throwing coppers on to the stage. After a pretty little tussle, the police turned them out.

Regarding these "hecklers", the Globe's manager, W. MacQueen Pope (1888-1960), told a different story, suggesting that Gaby, afraid of being rejected by some of her public as had happened in America, had engaged these trouble-makers as a means of getting the audience on her side:

> The pennies were thrown by five men in the upper circle who came in of set purpose to make a scene. We were aware of this and could have stopped them from entering. Gaby, who knew of it, said that if they wanted to come in they were welcome. I had a force of chuckers-out and policemen in attendance, and we had the gentry removed.

The most memorable performance of *Suzette* took place on April 20 1917—America Day—when Gaby appeared on stage as "The Quintessential Symbol of the Allies", in a sensational costume made by herself. The bodice comprised a tight sheath of French and English flags, and was worn under a huge, plumed Stars and Stripes cape. The headdress was even more spectacular—a three-foot tall arc of red, white and blue ostrich plumes upon which were set ten plate-sized silver stars. That evening, Gaby Deslys achieved heroine status, and the stormy applause when she took her curtain-calls lasted almost thirty minutes.

Gaby did not keep one penny of her salary of the profits from *Suzette*. Once she had paid the cast and technicians, and for the lease of the theatre, *everything* went to her French Soldiers Fund.

In the audience watching this final performance was Jacques-Charles, the man who had given Gaby *La Parisienne* fourteen years earlier. After being involved with many theatrical projects since last seeing her, he had enlisted to fight in the war, but had been discharged from military service after being wounded. He had recently taken over the lease of the Olympia—one of the few theatres in Paris still operating during the war. With him was Léon Volterra, the director of the Casino de Paris. Now France's leading revue writer, Jacques-Charles had recently completed *Laissez-les Tomber!* (*Let Them Fall!*), which he boasted would become the most fêted Parisian extravaganza in music-hall history. His original intention had been for this to be staged not at the Olympia, but at the much bigger Casino, with Mistinguett heading the cast. Volterra (1888-1949), was currently directing the ferociously difficult Miss in a revue and having a tough time of it. She was all for doing the revue, but only on condition that her current lover, Maurice Chevalier, should appear opposite her. Volterra could not stand Chevalier, and did not want him in his theatre. In a fix, Volterra and Jacques-Charles had travelled to London in the hope of wooing Gaby into appearing in their production. Because crossing the Channel was restricted for civilians, they had borrowed military uniforms from the Casino's costumes department and in Calais had boarded a steamer full of English soldiers heading home on leave.

After checking in at the Savoy, Jacques-Charles and Volterra headed for the Globe. The show had started, and they were asked to wait in Gaby's dressing-room, where they were confronted by her mother. Anna Caire listened to their proposition, and took the opportunity to persuade them *not* to hire Harry for *Laissez-les Tomber!* adding that she had never liked him, and that being with him—the endless arguments and making up—was taking a toll on her daughter's health. They were halfway towards agreeing to this when Gaby and Harry entered the dressing-room, arm-in-arm. Harry whipped off his shirt, and as soon as Jacques-Charles saw his gleaming, muscular torso it was love at first sight. The revue was discussed, with neither Gaby nor Harry showing much initial interest. *Suzette* was doing exceptionally well at the box-office. Gaby had Gordon Selfridge. Harry had Jean Maréchal. They were happy with things as they were for the time being. Volterra had hidden the unsigned contracts inside a bunch of lilies. After handing these to Gaby, he and Jacques-Charles left—but not before the latter reminded her of how he had helped *her* out, five years earlier, by defending her reputation—and that it was now time for her to return the favour.

The next day, Volterra received a call from Gaby, inviting him and Jacques-Charles to lunch at Kensington Gore. Harry and Anna Caire were conspicuous by their absence. When Volterra unrolled his table napkin, he found the signed contracts inside. *Laissez-les Tomber!* was therefore scheduled to open in December, six weeks after the proposed closure of *Suzette*. The title alluded to German bombs being dropped on Paris, and the Parisians going about their daily lives with as much indifference as they could. In the meantime there were two incidents. One made the headlines, the other was kept out of them.

Earlier in the year, Gaby had sat for an American painter named Ben Olchanevsy—the idea being that this would hang in the foyer of the Globe Theatre. Olchanevsky had asked for £20 for the work, which he had personally delivered to Kensington Gore. The press witnessed the event, and Gaby's claim that the woman in the portrait did not look remotely like her. She had kept the painting, and handed the artist £12, declaring that this was all that it was worth. Olchanevsky had subsequently referred the matter to the Small Claims division of the West London County Court—hoping that the resultant publicity would bring more commissions winging his way.

On 5 July, Gaby appeared in the dock, and the packed gallery and the crowd outside the court were treated to one aspect of her talent they had not seen before—her temper. It was a hot day, but she still wore her chinchilla coat, a huge hat, and a fortune in jewels and pearls. She explained to the magistrate, Justice Selfe, that she had refused to pay the full amount for the painting because Olchanevsky had not captured a suitable likeness—while her lawyer complicated matters by declaring that she had never sat for the painting in the first place—that the artist had copied her likeness from a photograph, and that his actions were part of a smear campaign that had followed his client across the Atlantic. Olchanevsky confessed that he *had* always been fascinated by Gaby, and that he had seen her several times in New York. Even so, the judge was not on her side. He ordered her to pay the remaining £8 owed on the painting, court costs, and undisclosed damages to Olchanevsky for attempting to ruin his reputation. Gaby left the court, struggling under the weight of the framed canvas, and when she reached the pavement asked one of the reporters if by any chance he was carrying a pen-knife. He was, and in front of hundreds of people she expressed her appreciation of "this piece of fucking shit" by slashing the canvas to ribbons. Ironically, Olchanevsky sold few of his paintings after that day.

No sooner had Gaby recovered from this ordeal than she returned home one evening to find the place ransacked. Despite her vast fortune the only staff who stayed with her overnight were her maid, who doubled-up as her make-up artist—and Elizabeth McDonald, a stalwart Scotswoman employed as her companion-dresser whenever she was appearing in England. Gaby summoned the police who initially believed the break-in had been perpetrated just to distress her, maybe someone who knew Ben Olchanevsky, as nothing appeared to be missing. Several days later she was interrogated by two Scotland Yard detectives, and informed that whoever had broken into her property had been working on information passed on to them by Madame Navratil—the woman who several years earlier in Vienna had claimed to be her mother, and who was now doing so again, declaring that Gaby's real name was Hedwige Navratil and that she had been born in Hungary.

This time the implications were taken much more seriously. Madame Navratil was Hungarian, and as this country *and* Austria were on Germany's side during the war, *had* Gaby been her daughter she would have been deemed an "enemy alien", as had earlier happened with Harry. Gaby and Harry explained what had happened in Vienna when this woman had turned up at the theatre, but this only aggravated the situation. The case was taken up by Basil Thompson (1861-1939), the Head of the CID and an intelligence officer with the Secret Service Bureau who in 1915 had been instrumental in bringing Mata Hari to justice. Initially it was suspected that Gaby's war work was but a front for her true activities as a spy, though this was soon disproved. Madame Navratil was again denounced as a fraud, and Thompson took steps to prevent the story from being published in the British press, though it did end up in some Continental newspapers.

On 13 October 1917, the curtain came down on *Suzette*, and Gaby threw a backstage party for the cast. Many of the chorus and bit-parts were feeling crestfallen, for with a war on they were unsure of finding work. Gaby came up with a solution for this. During the party she handed out pre-drafted contracts for anyone who wanted to accompany her across the Channel and appear in *Laissez-les Tomber!*

There was then a crisis, in the wake of the Navratil incident, when Harry was visited by the authorities, who had been made aware of his own Hungarian background. Not only was he blocked from crossing the Channel, he was threatened with internment. He decided that his only option would be to return to New York—taking Jean Maréchal with him. It was at this point that Jacques-Charles stepped in and promised to help, though this would come at a cost. And as Gaby's English fans waved her off at Victoria Station, little did they, J. M. Barrie, Gordon Selfridge—or she—know that she would never set foot on British soil again.

Stop! Look! Listen!

Fresh-air rehearsals for *Suzette* at Kensington Gore, watched by Gaby's dresser-companion, Elizabeth McDonald.

11: "Let Them Fall!"

When Gaby turned up at the Casino at the end of October 1917, she found the establishment being picketed by former employees of Léon Volterra's ex-partners Oscar Dufrenne and Raphael Beretta. The pair had brought these in after telling them that, with Volterra in charge, they would no longer have jobs. Gaby gave them her word that this would not happen—certainly while she was appearing at the Casino—and they quickly dispersed.

There were further problems two weeks later when Harry and Jean Maréchal arrived in Paris. Accused of draft-dodging, Harry was arrested and taken into custody. Hauled before a magistrate, he was charged with being a conscientious objector and told that he would be compelled to enlist with the American Army. A year or so earlier he had been more than willing to fight for his country, but since that country had made such a concerted effort to prove that he was not American but an enemy alien, this time he fought to evade conscription. Jacques-Charles stepped in, a good deal of money exchanged hands with the authorities, and Harry joined the rehearsals of *Laissez-les tomber!* without missing too many of them. In the middle of November, his brother Murray arrived from New York with his jazz-band, and it is interesting to note that Murray Pilcer encountered no problems obtaining a visa. For the time being, the Pilcers—along with Jean Maréchal and some of Murray's musicians—moved into Number Three, much to Anna Caire's distress, though there was some relief when she learned that Harry would not be sleeping in her daughter's bed.

The revue was assembled and rehearsed in mere weeks when workmen were still in the building. While Gaby and Harry took these teething problems in their stride, Léon Volterra fought to get the theatre prepared for the 12 December re-opening. Anticipating record audiences, he installed a cantilevered gallery capable of holding several hundred extra spectators. This was condemned as too dangerous by visiting inspectors, alerted by Raphael Beretta and Oscar Dufrenne in a last bid attempt to ruin Volterra completely. To prove that he knew what he was doing, Volterra arranged for a large bag of sand to be placed on each of the seats, and others were stacked in the aisles until the structure supported several times the weight of the proposed spectators—throughout the test, he sat in the stalls underneath it. The inspectors were given no option but to pass the structure, on condition that two additional pillars be installed for extra support.

During a break from rehearsals, Harry recorded one of his most celebrated songs. Fred Weatherall and Haydn Wood had written *Roses of Picardy* the previous year. Harry always sang it in English on the French stage, and in French when appearing in England and America:

>Nos chemins pourront être un jour écartés
>Et les roses perdront leurs couleurs,
>L'une au moins gardera pour moi sa beauté,
>C'est la fleur que j'enferme en mon coeur!

>(Our paths may one day be pushed aside
>And the roses will lose their colours,
>One at least will keep for me its beauty,
>It's the flower that I enclose in my heart!)

A century on, Harry's recording remains elusive, yet in the last two years of the war the song was so popular on both sides of the Channel that Jacques-Charles was compelled to include it in *Laissez-les tomber!* even though it did not fit in with the jazz-inspired scenario.

The revue cost so much to stage—the chorus line alone comprised 300 dancers—that Léon Volterra was already in financial straits before the curtain rose on the premiere. Gaby and Harry helped by allowing him to owe them their salaries during the first few weeks, and even invested money of their own to ensure that everything ran smoothly. They paid for their own costumes. This time the show-stopping routine was not *The Gaby Glide*, which was included in the programme, but a tableau entitled *Les Échelles*. This comprised a dozen 30-foot ladders strategically placed across the backdrop, from which descended a hundred-and-fifty chorus girls, naked but for spangled G-strings, high-heels and plumed headdresses. Nudes were not yet commonplace on the Parisian stage, and when Jacques-Charles asked Gaby to bare her breasts, she came close to walking out of the show. Despite her racy reputation, she knew where to draw the line. Harry on the other hand did not object to displaying as much flesh as decency would allow—his prime concern was his fear of heights when descending a ladder from the rafters.

Laissez-les tomber! will be remembered as the most famous of the Deslys-Pilcer Parisian reviews. It was whispered at the time that it would be Gaby's swansong. According to Professeur Gosset, the surgeon who had operated on her throat a few years earlier, she opened aware that she might have just months to live, and was determined to give the greatest performances of her life. She had an attack of nerves when informed that a large number of American soldiers were in the audience. The last thing she wanted was a repeat of the New Haven fiasco, though it turned out that she was worrying over nothing—they cheered her every move. During the first scene she materialised from behind an apple tree, covered in pink and white petals and singing Clifford Harris and James Tate's *A Broken Doll*, first performed by Tate's wife, Clarice Mayne. During the ladders tableau she wore a pink chiffon dress peppered with over a million francs' worth of diamonds, whilst Harry wore a Roman tunic, and was barefoot and revealing more of his thighs than would have been allowed on any Broadway or London stage. He and Gaby danced a brief adagio duet, after which the chorus girls, draped in black and white chiffon, descended to the stage to dance a dream sequence, their bare breasts and buttocks often swimming into view and bringing gasps of admiration from the audience. Then Harry unexpectedly danced out of his costume and, though not totally nude, the skin-coloured spangled slip he had underneath his tunic made him appear so to those sitting a distance from the stage.

The scene which caused the most fuss concerned not this sea of naked flesh, but Murray Pilcer's jazz-band, the very first such ensemble to appear in Paris. Unable to hear his musicians in rehearsals over the constant hammering of the workmen, he had brought in a range of noisy devices, including saxophone blasts and blank shots from revolvers. The first time these were fired, the audience panicked, thinking it was an air-raid. Then, as if by magic a huge staircase appeared, with Gaby and Harry standing at the top. This time she was drenched in carmine feathers and he wore tails. For more than thirty minutes, the pair danced up and down the staircase, performing perilous acrobatic routines and endding with the song that all Paris hummed during the winter of 1917/18:

>Y a du jazz-band le jour et la nuit!
>Y a du jazz-band, bonjour Paris!
>Y a du jazz-band partout qui rendent les hommes fous!

>(There's a jazz-band day and night!
>There's a jazz-band, Hello Paris!
>There's a jazz-band everywhere, driving men mad!)

Jean Cocteau, who admitted to having a crush on Harry, described *Laissez-les tomber!* in his bizarre, but inimitable way:

> The American band accompanied [Harry Pilcer] on the banjos and big nickel pipes [saxophones, not then widely-known in France]. To the right, in black clothes under a golden pergola loaded with bells, rods and motorcycle horns stood a black-clad barman. He was making cocktails, sometimes with a dash of cymbal, while mincing and smiling at the angels. Monsieur Pilcer, in tails, thin and rouged, and Mademoiselle Deslys, like a porcelain-complexioned ventriloquist's doll with corn-coloured hair and a gown of ostrich plumes, danced to this hurricane of rhythms and drums, a domesticated cataclysm of drumbeats which left them dazzled and drunk under the glare of six air-raid searchlights. Roused from its torpor by this extraordinary number, which is to the madness of Offenbach as a tank is to an 1870 *caleche* [one-horse carriage], the house rose and applauded.

As the air-raids became more frequent, the Paris authorities ruled that if the sirens sounded before 10 pm, all theatre performances would have to stop and patrons be given refunds. More seriously, to make up for any losses, some of the more parsimonious entrepreneurs did not pay the chorus. Volterra got past this by bringing the starting time of the revue forward by one hour, though there were so many curtain-calls and encores that the cast were often on the stage until well after ten, with the band making so much noise that on the occasions when the sirens *did* go off, no one heard them! If the show was aborted before curtain-up, while the other cast members fled to the safety of the fire-station in the nearby rue de Clichy, Gaby and Harry followed the crowd into the

Metro stations at Trinité and Liége, to entertain them there. When the air-raids became so frequent that the Casino could not open, those cast members with young families were invited to one of Gaby and Harry's "Métro revues", where the pair wore their everyday clothes on and entertained the children, handing out toys and sweets.

While they were appearing at the Casino, Gaby and Harry received a lucrative offer from Alfred Moul, in London. She turned him down, saying it was now unsafe to cross the Channel. Jake Shubert got in touch, and proposed the same terms as before for a season in New York—$4,000 a week, and half this amount for Harry. Her reply was that her fee had gone up, and that for her to risk crossing the Atlantic he would have to pay her a minimum of $5,000, while Harry had sworn never to return to the country which had treated him so abhorrently by declaring him an enemy alien. Shubert's response—that Gaby was demanding more than President Woodrow Wilson was earning—was met with a tarty, "Then get him to sing and dance in my place!"

What Moul and Shubert did not know was that Gaby's health was deteriorating, making long-distance travel risky. Besides one severe throat infection after another she was suffering painful attacks of rheumatism. Harry therefore opted to take matters into his own hands. Léon Volterra was told that when their contract expired in April 1918, they would not be renewing it. No longer Gaby's lover, he was the closest person to her in the world, more so than her mother whose hostility towards him was getting worse.

Early in March, while Volterra was still pleading with the couple to change their minds, Harry was approached by René Hervil, who had directed him and Gaby in *La remplaçant*, with a view to them starring in *L'ange de minuit*, which he would be co-directing with Louis Mercanton. The script, by Marcel L'Herbier, was based on his novel which had been translated into English as

The Angel of Forgiveness. Harry accepted on Gaby's behalf, hoping, as did her doctor, that several weeks filming on location in the clement weather would benefit her health.

Léon Volterra was faced with a dilemma. *Laissez-les tomber!* was sold out until the end of May, and he knew that only one star in France would be capable of replacing Gaby: Mistinguett, who he had just signed to appear in *Gobette of Paris* at the Ba-ta-clan. While Volterra accepted that Gaby was leaving the revue for health reasons, he failed to comprehend why Harry should wish to leave with her. Neither had he changed his opinion about Maurice Chevalier—he still could not stand him—while Miss refused to work without him, though by now their relationship was starting to cool. Volterra told Harry that he was willing to make a deal. If he submitted to an audition for Mistinguett—this was how *she* chose her leading men, as opposed to having them chosen for her—and if she approved of him, Volterra would up his salary by ten per cent! Harry went along with the idea to find out for himself if the 43-year-old star was as fearsome as everyone said she was. Miss later said she had been "knocked sideways and back again" by Harry's beauty. He was impressed by her, therefore it was agreed that he would film with Gaby by day, and still play the lead opposite Miss in *Laissez-les tomber!*

What Gaby had to say about the man she held dearest in the world working with a woman who never missed an opportunity to publicly insult her is not on record. The pairing with Miss was not to be just yet, however. When Harry arrived at the Casino during the last week of April to sign the extension of his contract and begin rehearsals, he learned that Chevalier had pipped him to the post, now that Mistinguett had decided to give her lover "another chance". The revised *Laissez-les tomber!* did not fare as well as the original. Though Parisian audiences worshiped Mistinguett, they were not keen on arguably the world's most famous dancer being replaced by a man who, though possessed of an enormous stage-presence, could not dance. Also the air-raids became more frequent. One occurred on the opening night, and was so frightening that the revue was re-baptised *Boum!*—a name which stuck until it closed on 13 June for the long summer holidays. So too ended the Mistinguett-Chevalier romance, though like Gaby and Harry the two would remain friends.

Shooting on the new film took up much of June and July. First up was a title change, when Harry complained that *L'ange de minuit* made Gaby sound like a prostitute—thus it became *Bouclette*, while it would be released in Britain as *Gaby*, and in America as *Infatuation*. Marcel L'Herbier had a bit part, and also in the production was Max Maxudian, who six years earlier had played opposite Sarah Bernhardt in Mercanton's *Queen Elizabeth*. The storyline was trite. Bouclette is an impoverished little flower-girl, down on her luck and shivering in her attic-room with only her poodle, Snowball, to talk to and share her misery and aspirations of becoming a famous café-concert *chanteuse*. This ambition is achieved without much difficulty, by way of an unhappy marriage with a man older than herself—played by Gabriel Signoret, who was only three years Gaby's senior. She becomes Flora Nys, tops the bill at the Casino, and halfway through the revue leaves her husband and begins an affair with a wealthy, handsome playboy (Harry) who showers her with jewels and other costly gifts. There is also a surprise ending, for instead of staying with her lover and shocking cinema-goers, she sees the error of her ways and returns to Signoret, her attic-room and her poodle—but not until she has sold her jewels to raise money to throw a Christmas party for the poor people in her neighbourhood.

Shooting wrapped, and Gaby spent several weeks resting at Number Three. Harry, after a tiff with Jean Maréchal, moved in— while Anna Caire moved out and returned to Marseille. Jacques-

Charles, hoping that Harry may have been "back in business", was a frequent visitor. Initially, Harry did not take his advances seriously, but when Jacques-Charles attempted to seduce him, he was shown the door. This caused some embarrassment when Léon Volterra commissioned the writer to supply an updated version of *Laissez-les tomber!* which he planned staging in Marseille towards the end of the year. Jacques-Charles' feelings would be still clear more than forty years later, when he contributed towards Harry's obituary:

> Harry Pilcer was tall, dark, mysterious and splendidly beautiful. He danced as naturally as most people breathe. I only wish that we could have got to know one another a little better.

On 18 August, Gaby, Harry and Léon Volterra travelled to Marseille. Anna Caire was now living in an apartment on the Promenade de la Corniche. Harry refused to even consider staying with her, and to avoid arguments Gaby rented two suites at the Hotel Noailles—one for herself, and the other for him and Jean Maréchal, with whom he had made up and who would be appearing in the new revue. Her mother's revenge was to tell the press that, for the whole of her career Gaby had been lying about her age. Gaby swore never to speak to her again, and for some time stuck to her word.

Marseille had been unaffected by the war and many Parisians who could afford the privilege had moved south, swelling the city's population by almost half. Not knowing how long the conflict would last—though she had decided to hang on to Number Three and Kensington Gore—Gaby began looking for a house close to where she had grown up. She settled on the Villa Maud, a small stuccoed Italian-style chateau on a raised position on the Corniche, overlooking the sea. It was only for rent, though the owner—an industrialist named Jean-Baptiste Ribaudo told her that it might soon be put up for sale. Therefore she took out a lease, a deal which set her back 500,000 francs.

Léon Volterra, meanwhile, had found a suitable venue for the revised *Laissez-les tomber!*—the Chatelet Theatre, on the Allées de Meilhan. Gaby had come here during her youth to see Polaire, but in recent years it had slumped in status and now put on boxing matches. Volterra acquired the lease for a song, and with lightning speed had it transformed into the 2,000-seater Grand Casino. This done, Jacques-Charles was summoned from Paris.

During the closing months of World War One, Marseille was a hive of sexual activity, its streets teaming with soldiers, sailors, and prostitutes of both sexes. Its night-life too was on a par with that of Paris. There were five major theatres, and innumerable *café-concerts*, *salles de beuglants* and *guingettes*—the popular dance-halls frequented by the working classes. Though Gaby refused to set foot in such establishments, Harry loved giving impromptu performances here, and was invariably asked to sing *Roses Of Picardy*. He was in his element, and he and Jean Maréchal were able to have their pick of the handsome young men found hankering around the street-corners of the Canabière. Even at the height of their affair, Gaby had never prevented Harry from making himself available to whoever had taken his fancy.

The rehearsals for *Laissez-les tomber* got under way during the first week of October, when Murray Pilcer and his musicians arrived in town. Anna Caire made a pest of herself by turning up at the theatre every afternoon and trying to tell Léon Volterra how to direct—until Harry gave him an it's-her-or-me ultimatum and she was barred from the building. Further problems arose when Volterra hired a local comic, Augé, to appear in the revue and inject a little humour. He was not a sensible choice. For years, he had been imitating Gaby, not as she was now but how he perceived she might have been had she never left Marseille and ended up down on her luck, looking bedraggled and working for a pittance in some tawdry dockside bar.

The revue opened on 14 November 1918, three days after the Armistice and ten days after Gaby's thirty-seventh birthday. The premiere was preceded by a victory parade through the streets of the city, which culminated with Harry singing *Roses de Picardie* to the ecstatic crowd—the first time he had sung to the French in their own language. Now that the war was over, he persuaded Jacques-Charles to re-christen the revue's most famous scene *Les échelles de la victoire* (The Ladders of Victory). After their first performance of this, Gaby returned to her dressing-room to find dozens of baskets of flowers, each with a card inscribed with the same message—"Affectuesement, Georges G." It took her less than twenty-four hours to determine the identity of her new admirer. He was Georges Gatineau Clemenceau, the 23-year-old grandson of the French president, Georges Clemenceau, newly hailed as "The Father of Victory".

Gaby invited Clemenceau to dinner next evening at the Villa Maud, after which she made the grave mistake of spending the night with him. Obsessed with her, he turned up at the theatre each evening with his rowdy friends, and they cheered her every move so vociferously that Léon Volterra received complaints that they were ruining the show for everyone else. On their first visit they released a hundred doves from the orchestra pit the moment that she made her entrance. On another occasion, while she was singing *Tout en rose* Clemenceau marched up and down the aisles, showering the spectators with rose petals. On another, the show was held up for thirty minutes when he presented everyone entering the theatre with a box of sweets emblazoned with Gaby's picture on the lid. The final straw came when he learned the name of her favourite perfume. Clemenceau bought dozens of bottles, which he and his friends sprayed around to an extent that the theatre almost had to be evacuated when some members of the audience started gasping for breath. News of his grandson's behaviour was relayed to President Clemenceau who, obviously remembering the Manuel affair, put his foot down and ordered young Georges to keep away from her.

A few days before Christmas 1918, Gaby and Harry gave an open-air recital—their first which was not an actual revue—at the Parc Américain, on the outskirts of Marseille. Though it was bitterly cold, more than 2,000 American troops turned up. A few days later, the couple began a tour of the local hospitals, and Gaby turned her home into an open house for wounded soldiers and their families. She told local reporter Jean Tourette that she was finding the revue too much for her, especially the ladders' tableau, and could not wait for it to close because she had received several film offers, one of which would be shot on location in Rome. Hinting that she might find love here, as had happened in Portugal, Tourette asked her about her affair with Manuel. Her response was a composed, "You mustn't believe everything you hear about *that* subject. Let me just say this—it's a legend that does contain a little truth, but *only* a little!"

Marseille was returning to normal. With the war over, those who had fled here from Paris and Northern France returned to their homes. Audiences were starting to dwindle, and in January 1919, much to Gaby's relief Léon Volterra announced, after the hundredth performance, that *Laissez-les tomber!* would close on 12 February. Then he offered a compromise. Jacques-Charles, commuting between Marseille and Paris, had whiled away the lengthy train journeys by working on a new revue, *On y va tous*! This would be on a smaller scale than the current one, but would feature Gaby, Harry, and Augé. Gaby was not having this. Augé's skits on her had become increasingly vulgar during the run of *Laissez-les tomber!* and she had no intention of working with him again. Volterra was told to fire him. He refused, and on the morning of 7 February—with six evening shows and three matinees left to run—Gaby and Harry boarded the Paris Express, leaving Volterra and Jacques-Charles in the lurch.

Jacques-Charles was so infatuated with Harry that he would have forgiven him anything, which also meant forgiving Gaby, who he believed had left her "coquette" days behind her and had a promising career ahead of her as a *chanteuse légère*. Not so Volterra, who vowed never to work with either of them again. He gave Gaby's part in the revue to Polaire—who by this time had lost her famous 18-inch waistline and resembled a gypsy, though her stage-presence was still formidable.

In Paris at Number Three, Gaby and Harry were approached by Bénédicte Rasimi (1874-1954), Polaire's manager and one of the toughest impresarios in the city, and now director of their former stamping-ground, the Fémina, which had been closed during the war and since been renovated. Rasimi had directed Mistinguett at the Ba-ta-clan, which she had taken over in 1911, and the pair had fought like cat and dog. She disliked Gaby, believing that her glory days were over, but recognized Harry's enormous drawing power. As he refused to appear without his partner, Rasimi put her prejudices to one side and engaged them to re-open the Femina. For the first time in their partnership, he would be earning *more* than Gaby.

Laissez-les tomber!

Gaby's villa, Marseille.

11: *The God of Luck*

La marche à l'étoile was scheduled to open at the Fémina on 30 March 1919. For the costumes, Bénédicte Rasimi commissioned Erté. Born Romain de Tirtoff in St Petersburg in 1892, this flamboyant, extroverted individual visited Paris for the first time in 1900 when his mother took him to the Great Exposition. Twelve years later, he made Paris his home. One of his first commissions was Mata Hari's legendary oriental costume which she wore in her play, *Marie Marais*. It was the *chanteuse* Damia, a woman with a penchant for Russians, who baptized him Erté—the French pronunciation of his initials. Erté worked for all the revue artistes of the day and also designed exotic underwear. Harry once sported a diamond-encrusted thong made by him. The Russian dancer, Ida Rubenstein, is said to have spent 30,000 francs a month, at the height of the Depression, on Erté-designed gold-leaf knickers.

By February 1919, Erté had moved to Monte Carlo with his Russian lover, Prince Nicolas Ouroussoff, throwing wild parties and entertaining a succession of hunky young men. They appear to have propositioned Harry, and been rejected. Therefore, when Bénédicte Rasimi contacted him and asked him to design Gaby's costumes for *La marche à l'étoile*, he refused to exert himself by travelling to Paris—if Gaby wanted to wear one of his costly creations, he pompously announced, *she* would have to come to *him*! Harry accompanied her, and made it clear from the start that he was not going to become another notch on the Erté-Ouroussoff bedpost. What is strange too is that Gaby, so used to having her photograph taken, very rarely posed in an Erté costume. We only know what they were really like by studying the actual drawings.

Rasimi's advertising campaign for *La marche à l'étoile* was bizarre, to say the least. The press were told there would be *three* leads—the third a "live gorilla". On account of low ticket sales because would-be spectators were terrified of it attacking them, this was demoted to a chimpanzee. Gaby dolls were commissioned to be sold in the foyer, while she and Harry flew over Paris in a light aircraft and scattered gold-foil medallions with their profiles. This offered Léon Volterra an opportunity to exact his revenge on them for walking out on him. His replacement revue with Polaire had closed after five performances. When the pilot was told to "go steady" because neither Gaby nor Harry had flown before, Volterra paid him to loop-the-loop above the Eiffel Tower and frighten them half to death.

The premiere took place on 8 April, delayed by ten days on account of Erté's refusal to come to Paris, and his lethargy when working on the designs for Gaby's costumes. There was a further setback when a thief broke into her dressing-room and stole a box of test-pressings of American songs which Gaby and Harry were said to have recorded in New York in 1917, the first time these had been mentioned. Why they were there, and not in the studio vault, was never explained. It may well be that Gaby was planning on singing one or more of these songs in the revue. What *is* known is that Rasimi was taking no chances where her voice was concerned—after she dried up during rehearsals, a gramophone was installed in the wings so that if this happened while she was on stage, she would be able to mime to *Tout en rose* and *La Parisienne*. An outraged Gaby declared that she would rather tear up her contract than do this. Fortunately she did not have to, as her voice was in fine form throughout the run of the revue. She offered a reward of 20,000 francs for the return of her recordings. It is not known for sure who stole them, though she was certain that Léon Volterra was behind the theft, and she may well have been right. They were never found.

For the first time, Gaby was slated by French critics for giving mediocre performances, though this was not her fault. The Fémina was too small for the extravagant kind of revue she was accustomed to working in, and ticket prices way too steep. There was a heated exchange between Bénédicte Rasimi and Erté when he finally arrived in Paris and observed that *her* name was listed in the programmes and on the posters as costume-designer. Turning the air blue, he threatened to remove his costumes and take them back with him to Monte Carlo unless the matter was resolved within twenty-four hours. A further problem was that Paris was still bustling with American troops, and that much of the revue's content was aimed at pleasing them and not the French, who wanted more *chansons* and less jazz. Harry's American songs, on the other hand—performed by a genuine American who did not keep forgetting or mispronouncing the words—were ecstatically received. Rasimi attempted to save the situation by asking Jacques-Charles to write a new repertoire for Gaby so that she could drop "world-weary" ditties such as *Broken Doll*. He refused, for no other reason than he did not have the time. He was about to accompany Mistinguett on her first trip to the United States.

Harry had by now come to the conclusion that his partnership with Gaby had run its course, and he was anxious to get away from her while the going was good. He was delighted when, half way through the run of *La marche à l'étoile*, she began an affair with Géraud, Duc de Crussol, who she had first met at the Casino de Paris in 1917. Sixteen years her junior, he was the son of Louis Emmanuel, the 14th Duc d'Uzès and Thérèse d'Albert de Luynes. But if his parents were initially indifferent towards the union, his grandmother was not. She was Anne, Dowager Duchesse d'Uzès, with whom Géraud lived at Dampierre, the family seat near Rambouillet in the Chevreuse Valley. Renowned as one of the greatest sportswomen in Europe and profoundly religious, she was a lieutenant of La Louveterie, the famous wolf-hunting pack, and owned 1,200 hunting dogs. Her husband had been killed in a shooting accident in 1878, since which time she had ruled over her family with a rod of iron. When news was brought to her that her grandson was having an affair with "France's most notorious showgirl", she ordered him to stop seeing her, which had the opposite effect—Géraud asked Gaby to marry him. Her response was that though she found the prospect of becoming Duchesse de Crussol most pleasing, she would still have to think about it.

La marche à l'étoile closed, and Gaby received word that the lease on the Villa Maud had ended, and Jean-Baptiste Ribaudo wanted to sell it. The asking price was 325,000 francs. Gaby called him, agreed to the sale over the telephone, and headed for Marseille. The papers were signed on 29 July, along with an agreement to purchase an adjoining small strip of land for a new driveway, so that the main entrance to the building would no longer be approached from the main road.

In August, Gaby returned to Paris, where she and Harry were contracted by Eclipse Films to make *Le dieu du hasard*. The director was Henri Pouctal (1856-1922), known in Europe for his *Count of Monte Cristo* serials made during the last year of the war. *Bouclette* had gone on national release, and was doing well at the box-office, applauded by the same critics who had panned the Fémina revue. During the first week of September, the pair travelled to Deauville, where the locations were to be filmed. Gaby had tried to explain to Géraud de Crussol how hopeless their relationship was. As with Manuel of Portugal, the class-laws of the day would have prevented her from marrying into the aristocracy *and* enjoying a stage or film career, and even had she retired from both she would have found it difficult to live down her flighty reputation, and would never have been accepted by a woman as discerning as the Duchesse d'Uzès. Pouctal was aware of this, and hoped that booking Gaby and Harry into a suite at the Hôtel Normandy might rekindle their affair, and reflect in their on-screen love scenes. Harry refused to stay here and chose a hotel in Trouville, within walking distance of the film set. Mistinguett had a country retreat at nearby Villerville, and it is believed that he slept with her for the first time here—his theory being that if Gaby could have sex with a much younger lover, then he could have sex with one a decade older than himself.

On the eve of shooting, Henri Pouctal laid down the law—his last film, *Travail*, had gone over budget owing to the tardiness of his actors. Everyone would therefore be expected on the set each morning at nine, to enable the beach scenes to be completed before there were too many tourists about. Harry was not required for the early scenes, or he almost certainly would have intervened. When Gaby suffered a dizzy spell on account of the cold and had to be taken back to her hotel, she sent a note to Pouctal saying that she would not be starting work the next day until noon, when it would be warm enough for her to go into the sea. Pouctal knew nothing of how unwell she was, otherwise he might have shown some compassion. One of the guests staying at the same hotel as Gaby was Lady Lilian Rothermere, the wife of the owner of the *Daily Mail*. With her was a tall, strapping 23-year-old bisexual Hungarian named Jimmy—listed on the payroll as her masseur, though when not tending to her aches and pains he rented himself out as a stud. Jimmy had also been hired as a bit-part in the film, playing a lifeguard. Lady Rothermere suggested that it might be a good idea if Jimmy went up to Gaby's room and warmed her up by giving her a massage. Clearly, she knew what this would involve, if the director did not. Guy de Bellet, observed:

> All the hotel chambermaids smiled at Jimmy while he smiled only at the bell-boys. He entered Gaby's room and

> set up his massage table. He always wore dark glasses when meeting a client. Looking like a Hollywood movie star enabled him to charge more for his services....Gaby pouted her lips, shed her transparent nightdress and stretched out on the table. Jimmy went to work on her, running his hands up and down her body from shoulder to hip, sliding them between her thighs...while her nipples swelled like strawberries.

De Bellet explains that at this point, the telephone rang. This was Harry, and the sound of his voice turned Jimmy on even more:

> Fugitive pleasure and gymnastics followed. "Lie on your belly," Jimmy told her. "Don't think about anything, only this!" And while he was deep inside her, for ten minutes Gaby forgot all about Deauville, the beach and the film...

The film's storyline was a basic treatment of good triumphing over evil. Gaby Balmacer is the unhappy wife of a dishonest banker—played by Félix Oudart (1881-1956), making his screen debut. He treats her harshly and she seeks solace in the arms of American millionaire adventurer Harry Duncan (Harry). When Balmacer is cornered after stealing her jewels, he commits suicide and Gaby gets to wed her sweetheart.

There were problems with the beach scenes. Harry was ready to face the cameras at six every morning, but Gaby refused to leave her hotel until ten. And still the director, crew and other actors were unaware of the reason for her "awkwardness", how it was essential that she should keep out of the sea until the sun had warmed it up a little. Her doctor had more or less passed the death-sentence on her, and only Harry and Anna Caire knew how really ill she was. Guy de Bellet continues:

The water was icy cold and Gaby was afraid of catching pneumonia. The director asked her to submerge herself completely, and it took so long for the "lifeguard" to dive in and "save" her that she almost drowned for real. The scene did not satisfy the director and he asked for another take, there and then, claiming that rain had been forecast for the next day. Minutes later she had an attack of sneezing, and by the time Jimmy had taken her to her room, she had developed a fever.

There is no doubting that shooting this scene—with at least six takes—hastened Gaby's end. Harry was at the Hôtel Normandy when it was filmed, meeting a British producer to discuss a proposed project to be filmed in London in the spring of 1920. He laid into Pouctal for not employing a stunt-woman, as a result of which after just three days in Deauville the director walked off the set and was replaced by 24-year-old Henri Diamant-Berger, who it emerged had been keeping Harry "happy" during their sojourn in the town.

When the locations wrapped, Gaby and Harry bid farewell to their respective lovers, and went their separate ways. While she stayed on in Deauville, he travelled to Paris, where the interiors of *Le dieu du hasard* were to be completed in October. Mistinguett tried but failed to get him to partner her in her new revue, *Pa-ri-ki-danse*, scheduled to open at the Casino at the end of November. She had commissioned Laurent Halet and Vincent Telly to write him a song, *Sur un air américain*, but Harry wanted nothing to do with this or the revue—his place was taken by Maurice Chevalier, while he and Jean Maréchal took a short break in London.

Gaby contacted Géraud de Crussol, and asked him to join her in Deauville. His grandmother found out, and more or less put him under "house arrest". Gaby therefore travelled to Marseille, where she and her mother—who not so long before she had sworn never to speak to again—fell into one another's arms at the railway station. Probably sensing that time was running out, the next morning Anna Caire accompanied Gaby to the offices of her lawyer, Maitre Maria. Here, she drafted and signed a will replacing the one she had made in New York. Her spirits perked up somewhat when she received a call from Baron Alberto Fassini, the head of the UCI (Unione Cinematographica Italiana). Having marvelled at her performance in *Bouclette*, he offered her a staggering 600,000 francs to appear in four films, which would be shot in quick succession between 1 January and 1 July 1920. Géraud de Crussol, on the pretext that he was visiting his sick mother in Paris, was allowed out of his "prison" at Dampierre, and accompanied Gaby to Rome. She signed the contract, and spent two days visiting the tourist attractions with her handsome lover, who proposed marriage once more. Gaby accepted—or so she told the Italian journalist whom she let in on her secret. This time, it was not the Duchesse d'Uzès that she had to worry about, but Géraud's mother. Thérèse d'Albert de Luynes had been content to allow her boy to sow a few wild oats with this "common showgirl", but marriage was another matter and she took out an order to have Gaby arrested and charged with abducting a minor! This was not worth the paper that it was written on. Gaby had not broken any laws, and Géraud was twenty-two and able to make his own mind up whom he wanted to wed.

Gaby's next move was extreme even for her, and doubly so on account of her failing health. Instead of returning to Marseille she made her way to Le Havre, with Géraud in tow, and they boarded the *SS France* for New York. There were no work commitments here, no contracts to discuss. She just needed to get away.

Géraud de Crussol

Le dieu du hazard.

Feeding the birds in *Le dieu du hazard*…

…and rescued from drowning by Jimmy!

12: The Fading Lily

The press reported that Gaby travelled alone to New York, and that Géraud stowed away on the ship. This was untrue—they were welcomed aboard by the captain, and several times invited to dine at his table. Their reception in New York, however, was not quite what they were expecting. Along with the group of reporters clustered around the gangplank were two plain-clothes detectives, here to arrest Gaby "for kidnapping a child"—and who were surprised to see her linking arms with a tall, well-built young man. No arrest took place, but they did have some bad news for Géraud. He was told that his mother, Thérèse d'Albert de Luynes, had learned of his "elopement" and wired ahead to announce that she was already at sea and on her way to New York to bring him home.

The press-conference which took place at the couple's hotel left reporters confused. Gaby first confessed that her lover *had* stowed away on the ship, then denied this, declaring that their relationship was legal and above board and that they had nothing to feel guilty about. She denied that Géraud had asked her to marry him, which he remedied by getting down on one knee and begging her once more to become his wife. At this, she laughed and told him to get up—though flattered by the proposal, she said, she was not quite ready to become Duchesse Gaby—and in any case, *no* man on earth was wealthy enough to purchase the freedom she had always enjoyed as a single woman. Then she changed tactics again when asked if she would be working while in New York. Dipping into her handbag, she haughtily read out the statement she had written on a sheet of *SS France* notepaper:

> I will not appear on stage any more here while the American public remains so cold towards me. I will only

participate in charity galas. Anyhow, I think it is time that I should be married. I've found the man I have always needed, and I am very much in love with him.

What happened when Thérèse d'Albert de Luynes arrived in New York is not on record, so there is no way of knowing if she met Gaby and gave her a piece of her mind. Géraud was banned from seeing her until 30 October, when his domineering mother allowed him to accompany her to the harbour, from which she sailed alone for Europe.

In Paris, through much of November between bouts of illness Gaby and Harry filmed the interiors of *Le dieu du hasard*. While in Italy, she had seen a film with Francesca Bertini, where the actress had committed suicide on a bed of roses. In Deauville, her masseur-lover Jimmy had told her after rescuing her from the sea, "Die at the end of your film, Gaby. If you do this, you'll be remembered as the most beautiful Marguerite Gautier of them all—even lovelier than Sarah Bernhardt!" The original closing sequence of the film, should have shown her falling ecstatically into her lover's arms with a promise of them living happily ever after. Now, a change was effected with Gaby scripting the scene herself. Touchingly, she writes Harry Duncan a farewell note, explaining that she cannot be with him any more because she only has a few weeks to live, and would not wish him to suffer watching her die. The tragedy is that she herself would not live to see the film in its edited print.

Jacques-Charles turned up on the last day of shooting, and made an attempt to reconcile Gaby and Harry with Léon Volterra. He had written a new revue, *Ca vaut de l'or*, which he suggested could be premiered in Marseille in January 1920, and spare Gaby the rigours of a Parisian winter. She was interested, but compelled to reject the offer having made plans to travel to Rome early in the

New Year to begin work on her first film for the UCI. She did urge Harry to accept Volterra's offer, and early in December he left for Marseille to begin rehearsals.

At the end of the month, Gaby was guest of honour for the premiere of Henri Bataille's play, *La vierge folle* (The Foolish Virgin), the inaugural production at the former Théâtre Rejane, recently acquired by Volterra and renamed the Théâtre de Paris. The press reported how unusually pale she looked under her make-up. When she left after the show it was pouring with rain, and hundreds of admirers were gathered outside the theatre, having queued for hours just to catch a glimpse of her. Gaby did not wish to let them down—drenched to the skin and refusing an umbrella, she spent over an hour signing photographs. The next morning she was unable to get out of bed and, thinking that she had caught a chill, Anna Caire sent for Professeur Gosset, who diagnosed pneumonia. She was taken to his clinic in the rue Antoine Chantin, where a more detailed examination revealed a small mass in her throat. Gosset advised her that he would have to operate, once her temperature had been brought under control, if she did not wish to risk permanent damage to her vocal cords, and she gave her consent.

It was much more serious than this, and Gaby is believed not to have been told how critical her condition was. Her mother, still holding a grudge against Harry, called Léon Volterra in Marseille and asked him to relay to Harry what Professeur Gosset had told her—that Gaby had a fifty-fifty chance of surviving surgery. He set off for Paris at once, accompanied by Jacques-Charles. When they arrived at the clinic they learned that Gaby had asked for one visitor only—Géraud de Crussol, now sitting at her bedside.

Over the next two days, hundreds of people visited the clinic, including Jean Cocteau and the composer Erik Satie. All had to make do with seeing Gaby through the grill in the door. She asked to see Harry, but her mother paid one of the nurses to ensure this did not happen. Mariano Unzué arrived from Vigneux-sur-Seine, and received the same treatment. When Anna Caire further announced that Harry and Mariano would no longer be made welcome at Number Three they headed there, where they felt they would be at least close to Gaby's aura, and had the locks changed so that *she* would no longer be able to get in. Matichon and her husband, en route from New York for an extended vacation in Europe when they received a wire from Anna Caire, arrived in Paris. They two were refused entry to Number Three, and were compelled to stay in a hotel near the clinic.

The operation took place a few days later. Vain until the end, Gaby would not allow Professeur Gosset to risk marring her looks by cutting her neck, and the scalpel had to be entered via her mouth. Because she was terrified of going to sleep and not waking up again, she refused to be given anaesthetic. Géraud de Crussol had not left her bedside for a moment, even when she had been undergoing surgery. It was he who defied Anna Caire's orders and allowed Harry into the room, where Gaby whispered that the operation had been a success, that she would soon be well again, and that he must return to Marseille where his public was awaiting him. He left the next morning, just hours before Gaby's health took a turn for the worst. Professeur Gosset had found the first operation so harrowing that, when he realised that further surgery would be necessary to save Gaby's life, he brought in a colleague, Docteur Martel.

A few days later, septicaemia set in, and Docteur Martel sent for a priest, Père Hennelique. Gaby was administered Last Rites on the morning of 9 February, and Harry was sent for. The next afternoon he and Mariano arrived at the clinic, where once again Anna Caire tried to stop them from seeing her dying daughter. The priest intervened, and this spiteful woman was banished from the sickroom. Not long afterwards, during the early hours of 11 February and with the three men she had loved sitting at her bedside—Harry, Mariano and Géraud de Crussol—Gaby slipped away. Mariano later published his memoirs in a French newspaper and recalled:

> I helped to embalm her, and even now I can see her in her glass-topped coffin. I dressed her in the Irish-linen gown she had worn the last time I took her dancing. I wanted to believe she was just sleeping, the little smile on her lips seemed to light up her lovely face. And she, who had adored precious stones, did not wear a single jewel in her coffin. I had locked them all away.

*

Gaby's funeral was as colourful as her life had been. Her body was taken back to Number Three and for two days lay in state in her sumptuous bedroom. Anna Caire took charge of some 10,000 floral tributes, most of which had to be laid out in the grounds. On the morning of 23 February, the cortege left the house, led by the hearse—this was drawn by two black horses, their bridles bearing Gaby's initials, followed by a horse-drawn carriage piled high with flowers. Driving his own car—a huge 30-horsepower white Sheffield—Harry led the mourners with Géraud de Crussol sitting in the front next to him. In an act of considerable kindness considering the despicable way she had treated him, he allowed Anna Caire to sit in the back. Behind them were Mariano, and dozens of Parisian show business luminaries including Léon Volterra, Jacques-Charles, Bénédicte Rasimi, Régine Flory, Max Déarly, Maurice Chevalier and Polaire. An estimated 500,000 people lined the streets along the funerary route. The service was conducted by Père Hennelique at the Church of Notre-Dame-de-Grace, in Passy, and lasted for over two hours. The glass top on the coffin had been replaced with a wooden lid, and outside the church this was removed and the coffin stood on its end so that Gaby's admirers could take one last look at her. This brought gasps not just from the 50,000-strong crowd, but from Harry and Mariano—someone, almost certainly Géraud de Crussol—had fastened a row of pearls around her throat, not just any pearls but those given to her by Manuel of Portugal.

Gaby's coffin rested overnight in the church in front of the altar, while the mourners returned to Number Three for the reading of the will, which she had entrusted to Mariano. The exact value of her estate was not known, but her properties and assets in France alone were estimated to be worth around 12 million francs—by today's figures, around £45 million. Her London lawyer later estimated that Kensington Gore and its contents, when sold, would raise enough money to buy a row of suburban houses. The bulk of her estate had been bequeathed to Anna and Matichon Caire, but with a codicil stressing that they would have to retain 75% of whatever they received and provide in *their* wills for the poor of Marseille. Gaby had also specified that her villa should be donated to the city after her mother's death, and be transformed into a hospice for sick children. Her greatest regret was that she and Harry had never had children of their own. Harry himself was left 1 million francs, a staggering amount, and an annuity of 18,000 francs to be paid to him on each anniversary of her death. He told the gathering that he would never touch a franc of this for himself, and this brought an angry outburst from Anna Caire, who threatened to take him to court for influencing Gaby while she had been dictating her will. In fact, they had been hundreds of miles apart at the time, and not on the best of terms. Anna Caire further criticised Harry for putting his career first, by returning to his revue rather than staying by her dying daughter's bedside—forgetting that *she* had banned him from the sickroom. She was unaware that Gaby had urged him to do this, after convincing him that she was getting better.

On the morning of 24 February, Père Hennelique read an address, while Gaby's coffin was being loaded into the hearse which would take it to the railway station for its final journey to Marseille. A special carriage had been constructed, with black satin-padded walls piped with gold. This was Gaby's ultimate gift to herself—she had insisted that her funeral should cost at least 20,000 francs, and that there should be no solemnity. The coffin was accompanied by Harry, Géraud de Crussol and Anna Caire—sitting with her back to them—and to prevent the press from taking photographs the blinds were closed throughout the entire journey. The carriage and its occupants remained in a siding outside the Saint-Charles station until the next morning, when the coffin was removed and taken to La Plaine, the square close to where Gaby had been born. It was raining heavily, but this did not deter the students from the Conservatoire from holding a public service which attracted 12,000 locals. 20,000 more were gathered within the St-Pierre cemetery, and as the cortege passed through the gates it was observed that the mourners were no longer headed by Harry, Géraud and Anna Caire, but by a half-grown donkey. For many years, the reason for this "in-joke" eluded even those press scandalmongers who had attacked Gaby for the better part of twenty years, and it was Mistinguett who solved the riddle. Gaby, after being seduced by Harry for the first time on the floor of her dressing-room in New York, had watched him crawling away on all-fours, and his "more than adequate endowment" had reminded her of the donkey kept by the sisters at the convent in Marseille. Gaby had repeated the incident to one or two friends who had taken her suggestion seriously—"If Harry can't be at my funeral, then please send the next-best thing!" Gaby was laid to rest in the tall, white marble tomb she had bought for her father—a temporary measure, until the mausoleum she had commissioned for herself was ready.

*

Géraud de Crussol, did not remain grief-stricken for long. He married Anne Gordon in 1923, and died six years later, aged thirty-one. Mariano Unzué ended his relationship with Arlette Dorgère and returned to Buenos Aires, where he died in 1936, aged sixty-two.

Anna Caire's spite and her disregard for Gaby's wishes knew no bounds. Harry commissioned a bronze palm to be placed on Gaby's tomb, which her mother removed and had destroyed—claiming that as he had bought it with Gaby's money (he had not) then, as Gaby's money should have legally belonged to her, she had a legal right to do as she pleased with anything that it was spent on. She contested Gaby's legacy to Harry, declaring that he had coerced her into bequeathing him 1 million francs and an annuity which, as her next-of-kin, should be hers. The action failed, but this did not lessen Anna Caire's hatred of him. She bribed the florist who had supplied him with two-hundred white lilies for Gaby's funeral to quadruple the bill—which came to a staggering 19,000 francs. The florist was arrested, and both he and Anna given police cautions. A feature appeared in the satirical publication, *Le Cri de Paris*, "King Manuel of Portugal's Interest In Gaby Deslys Was Not Entirely Quenched By Time". The writer added that Manuel's ancient seal ring bearing the crest of the Portuguese royal family and given by him to Gaby, had gone missing. Anna Caire accused Harry of stealing it, though it subsequently emerged that it had never left Lisbon.

When she learned that Gaby had arranged for the École de Beaux Arts, in Paris, to build her mausoleum and deduct the money from her estate—an estimated 500,000 francs—Anna Caire cancelled the project, which was already in construction. The establishment sued her for 80,000 francs, lost the case, and the mausoleum was never completed. The plot of land assigned to it was ploughed over, and Anna had it planted with the flowers her daughter had hated most—geraniums.

Anna Caire remained bitter towards those who had cared for Gaby until the end, dying in 1936, aged around eighty. Matichon died in 1951, when the Villa Maud was handed over to the city of Marseille to be turned into a hospice for children, as Gaby had requested.

Whether Gaby was buried still wearing Manuel of Portugal's pearls has always been hotly disputed. If they were removed, no one seems to know what became of them. What is interesting is that, after thieves tried to break into Gaby's tomb to look for them, their effort failed on account of the six-inch thick steel plate that had been placed on top of her coffin.

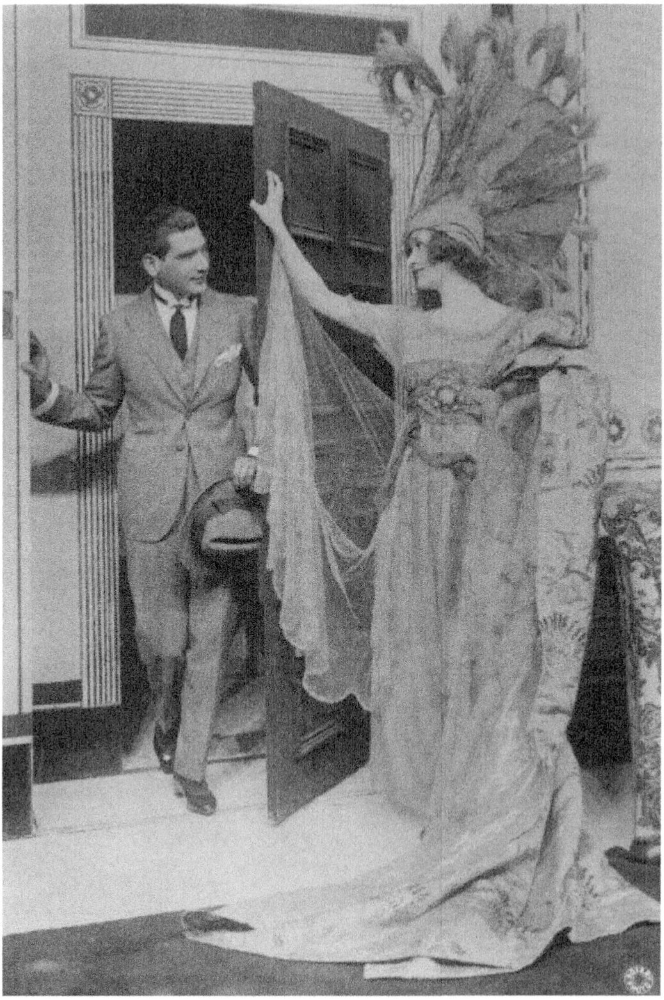

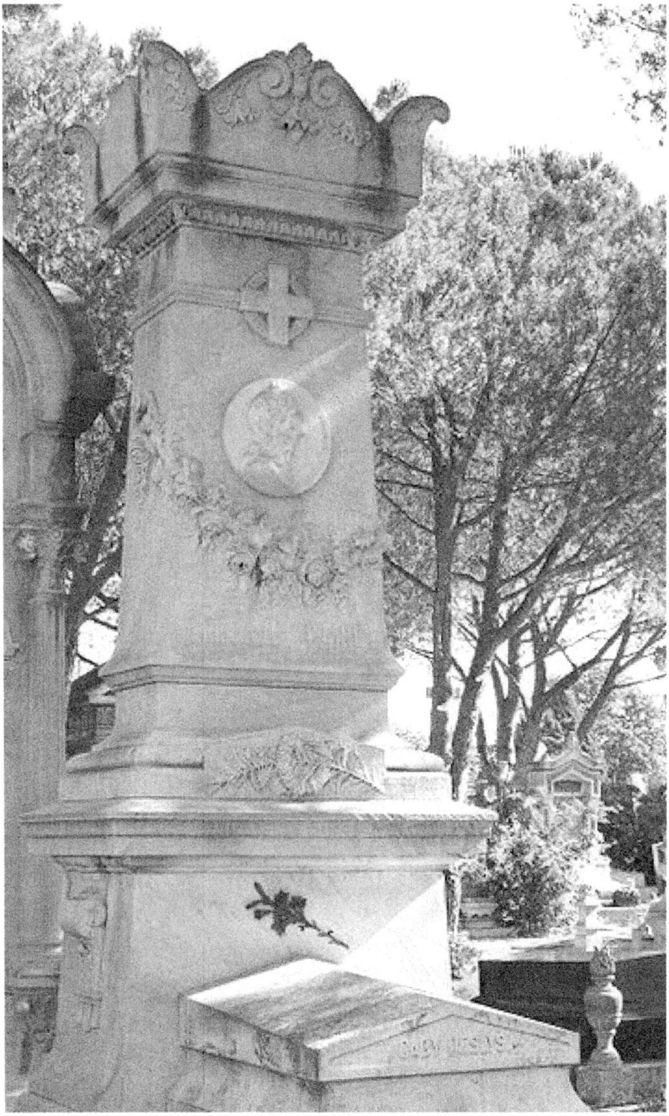

13: The Show Goes On…

Mistinguett is said to have been devastated by the news of Gaby's death. Though they had been rivals for a decade, Miss would never have wished Gaby harm, and always maintained that she preferred her enemies to be "alive and kicking" so that she could get at them. Her joke with the donkey at Gaby's funeral had not been appreciated by the Caires, and when Miss learned that they had turned against her "Hungarian donkey", she rushed to his defence.

As a tribute to his lost love, Harry choreographed and stage-managed a short season at the Casino, and in the second half of the programme danced *L'après-midi d'un faune*. When someone called out Gaby's name, he burst into tears and had to leave the stage. Soon afterwards he suffered a breakdown, of such intensity that it lasted off-and-on for another forty years. He stayed in Paris long enough to attend the auction on 28 June 1920 of Gaby's effects at the Hôtel Drouot. Exactly how much this raised was never made public. A triple-string of pearls allegedly given to her by Manuel of Portugal—*not* the ones she may or may not have been buried wearing—fetched over 1 million francs. At a cost of 30,000 francs, Harry bought many of these items for himself. He had ended his relationship with Jean Maréchal and moved into an apartment on the fashionable Avenue de Tourville, in Marseille, where he turned the largest room into a shrine for his great love. Mistinguett had bought several of Gaby's paintings, and she had one of these sent to him, which Harry hung over the altar here. He put in a bid for Gaby's gilded swan-shaped "Cupid's Target" bed when this was put up for auction at the Villa Maude, but lost out to Paramount Pictures, whose French representative offered Anna Caire $25,000 which no one could match. It subsequently featured in several Hollywood films, firstly in *Trifling Women* (1922), then more famously in Lon Chaney's *Phantom of the Opera* (1925) Carole Lombard's *Twentieth Century* (1934), while Norma Desmond slept in it in *Sunset Boulevard* (1950).

In 1943, MGM acquired the rights to Gaby's life story—one assumes from her only surviving relative, Matichon—as a vehicle for Judy Garland. Arthur Freed was hired to produce what was described as "a no-holds-barred account of France's most famous musical-comedy star". One may only ponder just how much of Gaby's real life was planned for the big screen—Harry Pilcer did not wish to be represented in it, and Freed declared that there would be no references to Manuel of Portugal or Gordon Selfridge! Needless to say, the project was cancelled and Judy went on to make *Meet Me In St Louis*. Gaby *did* feature in two scenes of *Deep In My Heart* (1954) the highly-fictionalised story of the compose Sigmund Romberg, where she was woefully portrayed by the Russian actress-dancer Tamara Toumanova—of which the least said, the better.

Harry's mental state deteriorated to such an extent in the months following Gaby's death that he twice attempted suicide. Jacques-Charles had given up trying to seduce him, and the two were now friends. When he called on him one morning unannounced, with a script he had written for a new revue, he found him slumped in an armchair after taking an overdose of barbiturates. The speedy arrival of a doctor saved his life, and when Jacques-Charles called Mistinguett to explain what had happened, she instructed him to bring Harry back to Paris at once. For several weeks, they retired to her retreat at Villerville, near Deauville in Normandy. Here, far from the prying eyes of the press, she set about nursing him back to health.

Psychoanalysts might agree that a sensitive man like Harry contributed more to Mistinguett's wellbeing than the egotistical Maurice Chevalier. He was never condescending or demanding—

and because he was as wealthy and almost as famous as she was, he had no need to use her as a stepping-stone, as many did, to further his career. He was able to penetrate her psyche and discover her almost childlike vulnerability. The events of his unconventional early years had not always placed him in a favourable light with critics and even Miss once confessed that she had only tried to woo him away from Gaby to make Chevalier jealous. She subsequently revoked that statement, but this did not prevent the rumour from circulating that she had taken advantage of her rival's death to grab him before someone else did.

Harry's second suicide bid occurred while he was staying with Miss, with barbiturates that her doctor had prescribed for his depression. Rather than summon help and run the risk of the story hitting the press she pumped his stomach and did not leave his side for a week. She, who until now had treated her men like doormats, slept on the floor next to his bed, and when he was strong enough drove him to her Paris apartment, on the boulevard des Capucines. Here, he found himself to be in good company.

The costume designer Charles Gesmar (1900-28) was a talented but highly-strung individual who at fifteen had left his native Nancy for Paris, armed only with a box of crayons and an exercise book for his designs. He had been taken in by Andrée Spinelly, an actress friend of Gaby and Mistinguett, and had subsequently designed the latter's costumes for *Pa-ri-ki-ri*. Spinelly had evicted him when, after a tiff with his current boyfriend and high on opium—his favourite "indulgence" since the age of seventeen—he had attempted to put a bullet through his skull in her bedroom but succeeded only in shattering her favourite antique vase. With nowhere else to go, he had turned up at Mistinguett's apartment, and within days she had unofficially adopted him, though it was *she* who, for the rest of his short life, called *him* "Maman". She observed in her memoirs:

Gesmar was so delicate, and so feminine, one angry word would have broken him in half. He loved to poke fun at the "real" men of the music-hall—the virile types who had everything down below, but nothing at all up top. He worked his fingers to the bone, and frittered away a fortune. He never paid a taxi-driver with anything less than a hundred-franc bill, and he *never* asked for the change!

For Harry and Gesmar, fifteen years his junior, it was love at first sight. Miss wholly accepted this, so long as Harry graced her bed with his presence every now and then. As a declaration of her love and admiration for him, she wrote (and in 1936 recorded and sang in her only sound film, *Rigolboche*) a tender, heartfelt ballad:

> Au fond de tes yeux que je contemple avec ivresse,
> Je devine mieux ce que tu penses, mon amour.
> Je vois un peu de peine et même un gros chagrin.
> Je découvre des pleurs parfois que tu retiens...

> (Deep in your eyes, which I study with rapture,
> I better work out what you're thinking, my love.
> I see a little pain and even great grief.
> Above all I discover the tears you're holding back...)

Jacques-Charles was touched by Mistinguett's motherly devotion towards Harry, more envious that he was alternating between sharing her bed and Gesmar's, and not his. He made up for his disappointment by collaborating with Albert Willemetz and Maurice Yvain on the pastiche which became her theme, and which was later picked up in its English adaptation by Fanny Brice, Billie Holiday, and by Barbra Streisand in *Funny Girl*:

> Sur cette terre, ma seule joie, mon seul bonheur
> C'est mon homme!
> Quand il m'dit "Viens!" j'l'suis comme un chien!
> J'sens qu'il me rendrait infâme,
> Mais je n'suis qu'une femme,
> Et j'l'ai tellement dans ma peau!
>
> (My only joy and happiness on earth is my man!
> When he says "Come!" I follow him like a dog,
> I feel he would make me infamous,
> But I'm only a woman, and I've got him under my skin!)

Harry's affair with Gesmar was short-lived—not surprising as he always disliked blatantly effeminate men—though they remained friends. He and Mistinguett opened in *Paris qui jazz*—a revue in two acts, co-produced by Léon Volterra, Jacques-Charles and Albert Willemetz—at the Casino on 6 October 1920. Their co-stars were Louis Boucot and Jenny Golder, of whom more later. In one tableau Mistinguett interpreted Rose, a character named after the Coté perfume. Her Erté costume was one of the most stunning she ever wore, comprising 10,000 artificial roses whose "dewdrops" were genuine diamonds, and would be unaffordable by even the most affluent of today's theatre producers. In *Le Cirque*, Harry played Charlie Chaplin—while in *Le Harem* he played Ali Baba and Sinbad the Sailor to her Scheherezade. The show-stopping numbers were Mistinguett's *Mon homme*, which she crooned to him with a genuine sob in the voice—and Harry's French adaptation of George Gershwin's *Swanee*. Al Jolson had recorded this earlier in the year.

    Harry stayed with Mistinguett until the autumn of 1921 when he was asked to appear with her in *Paris en l'air*, scheduled to open at the Casino on 21 October. He turned the offer down when he received a cable from Jake Shubert, in New York, inviting him to head the cast of *Pins and Needles*. Gaby's death had settled their differences and much as he hated letting Miss down, he believed that a change of scenery, and country, would benefit his anxious state of mind. This opened at the Shubert Theatre on 1 February 1922, with British stars Nervo and Knox (later one-third of the Crazy Gang) and Maisie Gay supporting. Sadly, many critics never gave it a chance—awarding it a thumbs-down *before* the premiere, with *Variety*'s Alan Dale leading the charge and proving that he still held a grudge. Based on the book by Albert de Courville and Edgar Wallace, it had first seen the light of day at the Palace in London, and Rupert Hazell's original libretto had not been Americanized. Thus, while anglophiles such as the editor of the *New York Globe* applauded it for being "English as crumpets or cricket or a Saturday night in Piccadilly", the *New York Times* denounced it as "a generally ingratiating pot-pourri of nonsense". And if Dale praised Maisie Gay and hailed her "the new Marie Dressler", what he said about everyone else was truly spiteful:

> All those interested in the sublime art of musical-comedy will do well to see *Pins and Needles*. These gentlemen may then learn how *not* to do things: how *not* to write a book, how *not* to interpolate music, how *not* to joke jokes, how *not* to choose pretty damsels, how *not* to stage effects—in fact, how *not* to produce musical-comedies. The list of authors, sponsors, head cooks and bottle-washers for this revue is as extensive as a telephone directory but it would be a waste of time to quote them. As for Harry Pilcer—he will never be called a singer by any vocal lady, and there are such things, I think, as anaesthetics.

Suffice to say, when *Pins and Needles* closed after 46 albeit sell-out performances, Harry was in no hurry to appear in another revue in New York *or* Paris. Returning to Marseille, he kept a low profile for the next four years. There were countless offers of work from both sides of the Atlantic, calls from Mistinguett, and visits from Jacques-Charles, none of which tempted him out of his self-enforced solitude. In August 1925 he received word that his mother had died in a New York sanatorium. He did not attend her funeral, but donated the $600 she bequeathed him to charity. At the end of the year he travelled to London to spend time with his brother Murray, now living on Southampton Road. It was he who coerced Harry into returning to the stage, early in 1926.

Murray Pilcer had adapted *La Marseillaise* to his own personal style, complete with saxophone blasts, car-horns, revolver shots and the like. When his sister Elsie arrived in London with Dudley Douglas, now her fiancé, the scene was set for all three Pilcers to head for Paris, where they opened at the Empire on 30 January. The consequences were dire. During the first few minutes of the tableau containing the anthem the more patriotic members of the audience stood to attention, but as soon as they heard the syncopated sounds from the brass section, accompanying Harry and Elsie's off-beat shuffle which quickly developed into a series of acrobatic contortions, they began heckling. They and the other dancers were pelted with anything that came to hand—shoes, coins, cigarette-lighters—and when these were flung back, a riot broke out and the police were called. Fifty people were arrested, and twenty more taken to hospital, though none of their injuries were serious. The next day, the Pilcers were presented with an order forbidding them from ever staging the piece again in France.

Harry had more or less always got on with Mariano Unzué, who since returning to Buenos Aires had opened a theatre in the city. The Pilcers were invited to play a season here, with Murray combining his band with that of Juan Carlos Cobián, Argentina's legendary tango composer. Their shows were so well-received that the two-weeks contract was extended to three months, and led to the Pilcers and Cobián being offered a season in a revue at the New York Palace. Harry had not forgiven the critics here for savaging *Pins and Needles*, and turned the offer down. He headed a vaudeville bill on 14 June 1926, the reviews for which were so glowing that offers to appear on Broadway came flooding in. He rejected them all, his excuse being that he had to return to France to begin a new venture as proprietor of a casino—the Acacia Club in Paris was a temporary deal which nevertheless earned him a great deal of money. He then signed a contract with Oscar Dufrenne, Léon Volterra's greatest enemy, to appear at the Palace Theatre in *La Palace aux Femmes,* co-produced by Henri Varna and Oscar Dufrenne, with Jenny Golder as *meneuse de revue.*

Though Harry was primarily attracted to men, besides Gaby Deslys and Mistinguett there were other women. Golder (1894-1928) was born Rosie Sloman in Kyneton, Australia, and moved to Brighton with her family when young. At eighteen she married the dancer-acrobat Joe Bowden—as the acrobatic duo Jenny and Joe they made their stage debut at London's Continental Music Hall in 1914. The couple separated soon afterwards, and nothing more is recorded of her until she reappeared as Jenny Golder (her mother's maiden-name) dancing at the Savoy Hotel in Brussels. Here, she was "spotted" by Jacques-Charles, and brought back to Paris. With large eyes which made her appear as if she was about to burst into tears, and with her fabulous legs, at the time she became involved with Harry she was a serious contender for Mistinguett's crown. Indeed, in some revues Jacques-Charles perhaps unwisely billed her as "The Woman With Max Linder's Eyes And Mistinguett's Teeth". Needless to say, the older star loathed her and tolerated her presence in *Paris qui jazz* so that she could insult her each time they met backstage. Harry had obviously been attracted to Golder then, but had wisely kept his distance—Miss enraged is said to have been an extremely unpleasant experience. Now, and with Jean Maréchal out of his life for good, there was nothing to hold Harry back.

La Palace aux Femmes opened on 11 September 1926, and as its title suggests was initially little more than a display of legs, breasts and feathers, offering little in the musical sense. Matters improved slightly when Harry persuaded Varna and Dufrenne to include several American songs recently adapted into French, as opposed to the regular clutch of mostly forgettable ditties common to such productions. The show-stopper was Harry's rendition of *Toujours*—Irving Berlin's *Always*, which Berlin wrote as a gift for Ellin McKay, whom he married earlier that year. Jenny Golder's big production number, which saw the entire 300-strong cast crowding on to the stage, was Isham Jones's *I'm Tired of Everything But You*. Harry and Golder also introduced the Black-Bottom to Parisian audiences—causing such cheering and stamping of feet that it had to be repeated on the evening of the premiere. There were wolf-whistles from his legion of gay fans when, in one tableau, he wore skimpy skin-coloured shorts which from the galleries made him appear naked.

As the revue drew to a close, Harry asked Oscar Dufrenne's permission to take a fully-clothed version of the show on a tour of France and Germany—adding that this would culminate in a state performance before President Ebert and an audience of 14,000 at the huge Berlin Sportpalast. Dufrenne was against the idea until Harry promised to make good any losses incurred. When the tour proved successful the wily entrepreneur boasted to the press that the idea of taking *La Palace aux Femmes* on the road had been entirely his and Henri Varna's:

America has dominated our music-halls for too long. We believe the era of nakedness is over and we're anxious to show the world that a real French revue is possible without undressed acts as a feature. So, realising the most critical audiences would be those composed of Germans, we decided to stage the show in Berlin.

Harry *reciprocated* by financing the Berlin season himself, and pocketing *all* the profits. It proved the biggest money-spinner of his career, though he later said it had felt strange being robbed of his "freedom of expression"—in other words, his usual display of overt narcissism. German audiences heard *Swanee* for the first time, though he was not permitted to sing *Roses Of Picardy* as this was a symbol of those who had won the war. He sang and recorded Franz Bendel's turn-of-the-century classic, *Wie beruhrt mich wunsersam*, though the recordings of this and its English-language version, *Wondrous Is The Power*, appear to have disappeared.

It was at this time that Harry, at forty-one, introduced a new routine that most men half his age would have found difficult to execute—his "Drunk-As-A-Lord" sketch, choreographed to *The Coldwater Rag*, a syncopated piano-piece composed by Mollie Cloud in 1913. This saw him dancing backwards up a staircase—in precisely four minutes while undressing down to his undershorts and vest *and* drinking a bottle of champagne! And to prove that what he was quaffing *was* real champagne, he always saved a glass to pour and serve to a member of his stupefied audience.

Touring did not suit Jenny Golder, who became even more neurotic than Harry's former partner Teddie Gerard once the company left Paris, unable to perform without a regular diet of alcohol and pills. Unable to cope with her mood-swings, after the Berlin show Harry ended their relationship and hooked up with the show's third lead, 32-year-old Adrien Lamy (1894-1940). The pair were in their element revelling in the decadence of the Weimar Republic, engaging in any number of post-show trysts with young men they picked up during the course of the evening. Jenny Golder returned to Paris, and the consequences of this would prove dire.

Charles Gesmar.

Gaby's bed, which appears in *Sunset Boulevard*.

Mistinguett and Harry.

Harry and Jenny Golder…

…and in Berlin in 1927, with Jenny Golder and the actor, Spadaro.

Epilogue: Berlin...and Beyond

When Harry was offered a season touring the clubs and music-halls in and around Berlin, he held auditions for a new partner and chose Renée Sella, an exiled ballerina, then enjoying enormous popularity in Berlin. With her he danced *L'après-midi d'un faune*. The couple posed for the popular magazine *Elegant Welt*, with Sella wearing a tutu and Harry hovering over her, decked out in a silk and lace suit surmounted by an outspread gold lame cape! He wore this during one of his evening sorties with Adrien Lamy, and caused such a sensation that he was offered vast fees by several of the city's leading fashion houses to promote their latest way over the top designs.

When a photographer hired by the Salon Gustave asked Harry what he wore within the privacy of his bedroom, he replied, "Nothing. Pyjamas are not for wearing in bed, but for going out in." This resulted in him promoting their new range of "Mandarin" lingerie for men—sequined posing-pouches, see-through sparkling nightshirts and caped pyjamas. Harry turned up at one Berlin gay club wearing baggy pink and silver pyjamas with gold lame ties, over which he had draped a matching wrap which trailed seven feet behind him. He also modelled a lime-green ensemble which, with one tug of a concealed cord, rendered him naked!

Harry and Adrien Lamy returned to Paris shortly after the Christmas of 1928, and went their separate ways. Lamy forged a moderately successful career as an actor and singer—in 1930 he and Joséphine Baker recorded "J'ai deux amours", which was a massive worldwide hit. In July 1940, he and his better-known actor father Charles were killed when the Germans bombed Orléans, during the Battle of France.

On 27 February 1928, Charles Gesmar died, aged just twenty-seven. A common cold had turned into pneumonia, virtually overnight, and the flamboyant designer died in his sleep. Mistinguett later said that losing him had been the saddest episode in her entire life, and that she had loved him as much as her own son. Harry always called him "little sister", even when they were lovers. The funeral was gay in every sense. Many of the mourners—including Jean Cocteau, the comedian Mayol and Louis Leplée, the man who discovered Edith Piaf—turned up in drag. As the coffin was lowered into the ground one of Gesmar's friends stepped forwards and with a wild theatrical gesture sprinkled confetti into the void. Others threw streamers and tossed balloons into the air while Harry and Mistinguett sang *Mon homme*, before dancing the *apache* at the graveside.

Such hilarity aside, Gesmar's death hit Harry hard a few days later when he returned to Marseille, to another spell of self-enforced solitude and deep depression. This was broken twice—firstly when Jenny Golder called him to announce that she had ruptured a tendon in her knee and that she would be out of action for a while, then when she attempted to blackmail Harry into going back to her by vowing to kill herself if he did not. She had already given Oscar Dufrenne the same ultimatum, should he not put the two of them into a revue once she had recovered from her injury. One assumes that they called her bluff. On 12 July 1928 she was found dead in her apartment on the rue Desaix, having shot herself through the heart. Whereas the theatrical elite had attended Gesmar's funeral, hardly anyone was in attendance when Golder was cremated at Courbevoie, on the outskirts of Paris.

In January 1929, Harry went to see Marie Dubas (1894-1972), appearing at the Concert Mayol in Oscar Dufrenne's revue, *En pleine jeunesse*. Also on the bill was Lucienne Boyer, who the following year would have an immense success with the song, *Parlez-moi d'amour*. Harry had always admired Marie, known as

La Fantaisiste des Années Folles, one of the most respected and loved entertainers of her generation . In many ways she was like her friend, Britain's Gracie Fields, in that she had an uncanny knack of being able to switch from buffoonery to intense drama within the space of a song. Her most famous songs were *Pédro*, a hilarious number about a clumsy, randy matador—and *La prière de la Charlotte*, which tells the harrowing story of the pregnant girl who goes to Notre Dame on Christmas Eve to beg the Virgin Mary to allow her to die so that her child will not suffer the way she has her whole life. Tired of being partnered with temperamental women, Harry told Marie of his dream to work with her some day in a revue, and this came about courtesy of Léon Volterra. Such was Marie's innate charisma—not to mention that everyone in the music-hall adored her—that when Volterra signed her up for *Paris qui charme* and asked her to select her own partner and she chose Harry, Volterra offered no opposition despite their former animosity towards one another.

The revue was by Albert Willemetz and the actor-singer-songwriter Saint-Granier (1890-1976), much in demand at the time after adapting Mabel Wayne's *Ramona* into French. It would be Volterra's last revue here, for soon afterwards he sold the venue back to Henri Varna and Oscar Dufrenne. It opened on 28 May 1929, with a cast of 750, to the largest ensemble to have appeared on a Paris stage. The show-stoppers were Marie's *Les housards de la garde* and the raunchy *Femme du roulier*, traditional songs arranged by her pianist, Ralph Carcel. Harry performed his drunk routine, accompanied by Fred Mélé and his Sinfonic Jazz-Band. Each evening he brought the house down with *Swanee*—and with his own arrangement of Jame's A. Bland's 1878 classic, *Virginny*:

    Carry me back to old Virginny,
    There's where the cotton and the corn and 'taters grow!

There's where the birds warble sweet in the Springtime,
That's where there's love and my Old Sweet Home!

Though there would be other love affairs, Harry never stopped living in the past—dwelling upon how his life might have been had Gaby lived, had he not broken up with Jean Maréchal. His edginess throughout the run of *Paris qui charme* stemmed from the resurgence of the Navratil scandal courtesy of an "exclusive" in *Bruxelles Soir*, published in March 1929 but which only reached him a few days after the premiere, and the press intrusion which followed. In this, Jean Bernard claimed to have interviewed Madame Navratil, who still insisted that Gaby had been her daughter, Hedwige—that she had evidence to prove she had been adopted by Hippolyte and Anna Caire following the death in infancy of their own daughter, Gabrielle. Most French newspapers refused to run the story, but the British *News of the World* did. One of its reporters attempted to question Harry about this backstage at the Casino, and felt the might of his fist. It *was* subsequently proved that Madame Navratil *had* given birth to a daughter whom she had given up for adoption, though she had not been taken in by the Caires. What is remarkable is that when the Navratils were asked to provide the authorities with evidence of their daughter's date of birth, they supplied a document stating that she had been born on 30 October 1885. As previously explained, Gaby had been born on 4 November 1881, but had later knocked four years off her age. When her death certificate had been made out using papers from Number Three, 30 October had been copied on to it as her date of birth! Harry launched an enquiry. The real Edwige Navratil was found in Biarritz, and matter settled once and for all when she confessed that her mother had made up the story.

By 1930, Harry's career as one of the world's greatest dancers was almost over. Times had changed. At forty-five, many theatres considered him too old for the alarmingly acrobatic routines he persisted on performing, and refused to insure him. Also from this point he began suffering more and more periods of the darkest depression. In 1931 he was engaged by casino magnate Francois André as Master of Ceremonies for his establishments in Cannes and Deauville and later took over the casino at La Baule. British dancer Anton Dolin (Patrick Kay, 1904-83) frequently stayed with him, and may well have been an occasional lover. He recalled in his memoirs:

> When I was very small [sic, he was twenty-two!] my mother thought it would be good for my education to see Harry Pilcer do his drunk-dance on the staircase. Later, I got to know him well. He ran the Palm Beach Casino in Cannes, and whenever I wanted a table I just rang and he gave it to me...as I couldn't afford to pay those prices, I always went as his guest. He was a very kind person and we could all see why Gaby had adored him.

For years, there was speculation over how Harry stayed youthful looking, even in old age. His secret was revealed in 1946, when he played "Specialty Dancer" in the film version of Somerset Maugham's *The Razor's Edge*. Over the years, like Maugham, Noel Coward and Charlie Chaplin, he forked out huge amounts of money to have cells from sheep foetuses injected into his buttocks. As Maugham's biographer points out, "One of his greatest delights was demonstrating to his uncomfortable guests his ability, in his seventies, to achieve a rampant erection." Maugham also confessed, "One of my great mistakes was when I tried to persuade myself that I was three-quarters normal and only one-quarter queer, where in effect it was the other way around!" Harry had experienced few problems coping with his sexuality, and had never hid his light under a bushel. There were rumours that he and Mistinguett had rekindled their love affair—he was sixty-seven, she seventy-eight—when in the summer of 1953 she invited him to her villa in Antibes for what would be their final reunion. Harry and Miss hit the clubs and were seen be-bopping each evening, but it was her 25-year-old houseboy who kept him company when they got home.

Mistinguett told reporters at the time that Harry would always remain the greatest love of her life, even more so than Maurice Chevalier. She then almost counteracted the statement:

> But Harry doesn't want me, and never has. He's still got that woman's picture hanging over his altar. Harry never prays to God, only to Gaby Deslys. He spends so much time with the dead that he has no time for the living!

Mistinguett spent her last months at Bougival, where she died on 5 January 1956, aged eighty. Such was her importance that her body lay in state at the Madeleine, before her funeral in her native Enghien. Neither Harry nor Maurice Chevalier attended—Harry was seriously ill, Chevalier filming in America.

On 14 January 1961, shortly after performing a belated tribute to Mistinguett in a Cannes nightclub to honour the fifth anniversary of her death, Harry suffered a heart-attack. One hour later he was dead. His seventy-five years had been coloured with glory, and endless respect and adulation from those who had known him, on both sides of the Atlantic. A few days later he was buried in the Jewish section of Paris's Père-Lachaise cemetery, resting place of the famous. Along with Gaby Deslys, he was a pioneer, an icon who will never be replaced.

Harry and those pyjamas, Berlin 1928.

Harry: "Pyjamas are not for sleeping in, but for going out in!"

Harry, still looking incredible at 45.

Adrian Lamy.

Marie Dubas, at the time she appeared with Harry.

Cannes, 1947. Harry with opera singer
Grace Moore.

Bibliography & Sources (in order of appearance)

"Gaby Deslys em Lisboa", *O Mundo*, 15 August 1910.
"Gaby Deslys/ Rei Manuel Se Casar", *Illustracao Portuguesa*, August 1910.
"Gaby Deslys, Queen of the World of Art", *Tatler*, November 1910.
The Side Show, review. *The Brooklyn Eagle*, April 1907.
The Bad Boy and His Teddy Bears, review, *The New York Times*, January 1908.
Ziegfeld Follies 1910, review, *The Chicago News*, July 1910.
The Flirting Princess, review, *New York Dramatic Mirror*, 13 November 1909.
Bennett, James O'Donnell: *The Flirting Princess*, review, *The Record Herald*, September 1910.
Hammond, Percy: *The Flirting Princess*, review, *Chicago Daily Tribune*, September 1910.
Dale, Alan: "Mr. Harry Pilcer", *Variety*, September 1911.
Dale, Alan: *Les Débuts de Chichine*, comments, *Variety*, October 1911.
Deslys, Gaby: quote, *New York Herald*, October 1911.
Deslys, Gaby: "Response to Alan Dale", *New York Journal*, December 1911.
"Gaby Deslys and Harry Pilcer Married?" *Tatler*, January 1912.
Renaison, Paul (Jean-Ernest-Charles): "Gaby Deslys", *Gil Blas*, 21 June 1912.
Tove, Francis: "Fleur Deslys, At Whose Feet Respectability Worships", *The Bystander*, 26 July 1911.
Sherwin, Louis: *The Honeymoon Express*, review, *New York Globe*, February 1913.
Shaw, George Bernard: Letter in defence of Gaby Deslys, *The Times*, October 1913.

The Little Parisienne, review, *Manitoba Free Press,* November 1913.
"Gaby Deslys At Work For Famous Players", *Motion Picture World*, 15 August 1914.
"Gaby Deslys At Home", *The Sketch*, April 1915.
The Rosy Rapture, review, *The Times*, 23 March 1915.
"G. Is For Gaby! Saucy Suzette!" *The Sketch Supplement*, 7 March 1915.
Stop! Look! Listen! review, *New York Times*, December 1915.
Stop! Look! Listen! review, *Green Book Magazine*, 16 January 1916.
"The Cat & The Canary", review. *The Times*, April 1916.
Her Triumph, review, *The Otago Daily News* (Dunedin, New Zealand), 17 April 1916.
Dale, Alan: *Harry Pilcer Presents*, review, April 1916.
Dale, Alan: "The Gaby Deslys Boom", *Variety*, May 1916.
"Jingle", *Suzette*, review. *The Bystander*, 18 April 1916.
Cocteau, Jean: "*Laissez-les Tomber!* review, *La Sirène*, 1918.
Tourette, Jean: Gaby Deslys interview, *Le Petit Provençal*, December 1918.
Michel, Michel-George: Interview with Gaby Deslys, January 1919.
"King Manuel of Portugal's Interest In Gaby Deslys Was Not Entirely Quenched By Time", *Le Cri de Paris*, 1920.
Dale, Alan: *Pins & Needles*, review, *Variety*, February 1922.
Dufrenne, Oscar: *La Palace Aux Femmes*, quote to Reuters, January 1927.
Bernard, Jean: La Scandale Navratil, *Bruxelles-Soir*, March 1929.
Jacques-Charles: *De Gaby Deslys à Mistinguett*, Gallimard, 1932.
Unzué, Mariano: *Memoirs*, 1932. Quoted by Jacques-Charles.
Polaire: *Polaire par elle-même*, Editions Figuiere, 1933.

Lorrain, Jean: *La ville empoisonnée*, posthumously published 1936, Editions Jean Crés.

Gilbert, Douglas: *American Vaudeville: Its Life and Times*, Whittlesey House Books, 1940.

Macqueen-Pope, Walter: *Carriages At Eleven: The story of the Edwardian Theatre*, Huchinson, 1947.

Beaton, Cecil: *The Glass of Fashion*, Weidenfeld & Nicholson, 1954.

Mistinguett: *Mistinguett*, Elek Books, 1954.

Bellet, Guy de: *Gaby Deslys*, Collection La Vie Amoureuse, 1958.

Mackintosh, Alastair: *No Alibi: The Memoirs of Captain Alastair Mackintosh*, Muller, 1961.

Dolin, Antoine: *Last Words: A Final Autobiography*, Century, 1985

Bret, David: *The Mistinguett Legend*, Robson, 1990.

Goldman, Herbert G: *Jolson: The Legend Comes To Life*, Oxford University Press, 1990.

Bret, David: *Maurice Chevalier: Up On Top Of A Rainbow*, Robson, 1992.

Anonymous: *The Life of Jenny Golder*, RPM Reprographics, 2000.

Hastings, Selina: *The Secret Lives of Somerset Maugham*, John Murray, 2009.

Filmography

Animated Weekly, Number 55 (GD/HP)
Universal Manufacturing Company, 1913
Editor: Jack Cohn. Screened 21/23 March, this features newsreel of the previous week's headlining events: New York's St Patrick's Day Parade, Harry Pilcer and an unnamed partner dancing The Turkey Trot, etc. Gaby is seen meeting her mother, newly arrived from France. As such, though the footage has disappeared, it was the first time Gaby had appeared on celluloid.

La Remplaçante (GD/HP)

1914.

Directors: René Hervil, Louis Mercanton. With Gaby Deslys, Harry Pilcer, Jean Angelo.

One reel. No other details.

Her Triumph (GD/HP)

Famous Players (Paramount), 1915.

Producers: Daniel Frohman, Adolph Zukor. Director: René Hervil. With Gaby Deslys, Harry Pilcer.

5 reels. No other details.

Rosy Rapture (GD)

Neptune Film Company, 1915

Director: Percy Nash. Script: J. M. Barrie. With Gaby Deslys, Biddy de Burgh, John East. G. K. Chesterton, George Bernard Shaw.

Dress rehearsal for the London revue. One reel.

Bouclette (UK/USA: Infatuation) (GD/HP)

Pathé-Exchange, 1918.

Directors: René Hervil, Louis Mercanton). Script: Marcel L'Herbier. With Gaby Deslys, Harry Pilcer, Gabriel Signoret, Marcel L'Herbier, Max Maxudian. 5 reels.

Le Dieu du Hasard (GD/HP)

Eclipse, 1920.

Director: Henri Pouctal. Script: Fernand Noziere. With Gaby Deslys, Harry Pilcer, Félix Oudart, Georges Treville, "Jimmy". 5 reels.

Détresse (UK/USA: **Distress**) (HP)
1929. No company details.
Director: Jean Durand. With Harry Pilcer, Philippe Hériat, Maurice Luguet, Alice Roberts. No other details.

La Femme Revée (UK: An Ideal Woman) (HP)
Franco-Film, 1929.
Director: Jean Durand. Script: Perez de Rosas. With Harry Pilcer, Charles Vanel, Alice Roberts; Tony d'Algy, Thérèse Kolb, Jeanne Grumbach. No other details.

Thank Your Lucky Stars (HP)
Warner Brothers, 1943
Director: David Butler. Script: Norman Panama, Melvin Frank, James V. Kern. All-star production cast playing themselves included Humphrey Bogart, Eddie Cantor, Errol Flynn, Bette Davis, Olivia de Havilland, etc. Harry played "Man In Broadcasting Station). 127 minutes.

Cendrillon (Cinderella) (HP)
Forrester Parent Productions, 1937.
Director: Pierre Caron. Script: Jean Montazel. With Joan Warner, Christiane Delyne. Harry was choreographer. 95 minutes.

The Razor's Edge (HP)
Twentieth Century-Fox, 1946.
Director: Edmund Goulding. Script: Lamar Trotti, W. Somerset Maugham (novel). With Tyrone Power, Gene Tierney. Harry played "Speciality Dancer", and was choreographer. 145 minutes.

Printed in Great Britain
by Amazon